# Farm Life

# on

# Field and Fell

**Alfred Hall**

HAYLOFT

First published 2006

Hayloft Publishing Ltd, Kirkby Stephen, Cumbria, CA17 4DJ

Tel: (017683) 42300
Fax: (017683) 41568
E-mail: books@hayloft.org.uk
Website: www.hayloft.org.uk

ISBN: 1 90452448 6

A catalogue record for this book is available from the British Library.

For my grandchildren,
Gareth and Jilly.

# CONTENTS

# PREFACE

These stories are a commentary on the farming scene as it changed during the earlier years following the Second World War, when the power of the farm tractor was replacing the power of the farm horse.

The tractor also took over from the steam traction engine to haul and to drive the mobile threshing mill; then the combine harvester replaced both the self-binder mower and the threshing mill. Cattle which were not of a naturally polled breed looked unnatural without horns, and butter was churned on the farm.

Hay rakes, pitch forks, hay knives, draining spades, hedge slashers, sickles and scythes were becoming less essential handtools. Consequently, farmers' hands became less horny, freed from seggs, more tender and susceptible to blister. Henceforth, the work achieved with such handtools was to be undertaken by noisy machinery controlled by an operator seated comfortably in a cushioned tractor cab wearing lightweight shoes instead of sturdy hob-nailed boots.

This collection of stories is based on some of the author's original talks broadcast by the BBC during twenty-five years as a free-lance broadcaster on radio and television.

Then (before 1944)

# 1
# A Hard Winter

It seems a long time since the fields were bright with a golden harvest. Wherever you look, the countryside is locked in its winter retirement. No foliage, a brown bareness everywhere.

I remember standing on the stubble as the rising moon glowed like a red ball through the dew-laden evening air. It was the end of harvest. Quite an early finish. Bill climbed down from the stack he'd just finished, slid his jacket on with a shudder and said: "By gum, there's a touch o' frost!" And we had the notion that the early nip in the air was an omen of a long, hard winter.

Of course, it was only a guess. But one morning, I watched a high-flying flock of geese come inland from the north – and that set me wondering again. And, a few days later, chill winds blew, and robins came hopping round the yard – more friendly than ever. They fluffed out their feathers to keep warm, picked among the hayseeds, and were grateful for breadcrumbs. Well, those robins are still with us, and y'know, as they watch me breaking the ice on the trough in the yard on cold mornings, I can imagine them saying: "We told you it'd be a hard winter!"

Hard frost has laid up the plough and the ploughman has hitched his tractor to the manure spreader to take advantage of getting his loads on to the fields without the risk of bogging down. And the cowman has used his few daylight hours between foddering and milking time in helping to trim the hedgerows. But it's the shepherd who's spent most time out of doors. Twice a day, he counts his sheep. He has feeding troughs in the field, and his flock knows when to expect him. His collie gets little practice now because the sheep don't need to be rounded up. As soon as Shep, as we call him, opens the field gate, carrying his bag of crushed grain on his back, they all mill round the troughs. And they quickly eat up what he's brought for them. If there's one that doesn't greet him like this, it's very likely ailing, and he'll set about doctoring it. Of course, when there's snow, Shep has a busier time than ever. Then he must keep on carrying food out to those troughs because whilst the snow lies, there's no pasture to graze.

It's a good sign to see more sheep on the general farms. There they are – turning the grass and turnips into mutton. It's a good sign, because it shows good grassland management. There's nothing like the "golden hoof", as we say, for maintaining the fertility of the soil. When the grass and the turnips are eaten off – and when the frost isn't there – the plough will go to work on those fields, and, next year, they'll grow acres of golden corn. And next year's harvest will be the better for this year's sheep. Aye, there's truth in that old dictum which says: "There's nowt like sheep for making good corn."

# 2

## SNAGGING TIME

There's one job on the land that can last most of the winter – except, of course, when it comes to a full stop with hard frost – and that job is "snagging". In some places "snagging" is also known as "toppin' an' tailin'". What is it? Well, it's pulling turnips and chopping off the roots and the tops.

You see, snagging is a job that isn't necessarily finished before Christmas, although it's usual to get as many turnips as possible carted off and stored fairly early on in the winter – especially when they're for cattle feed. Well, to carry out this snagging business you've got to use a chopping tool which is like a short sickle. And this is the drill: You pull up a turnip with one hand; then, using the "snagger", as we call it, in the other you chop off the root; then with another quick flick you chop off the top which you are holding in your hand and the turnip itself drops to one side. Now, you've got to be rather smart to do this properly – you've got to be a good shot! It's never long before a fellow whose new to snagging makes a bad shot and hacks a lump out of his index finger! Believe me, after he's done that his skill as a snagger improves enormously!

Out in the middle of a turnip field you've no shelter. A cold thin wind cuts right through you, your boots become heavier with sticky mud and every now and again you straighten up your stiffened back for ease and wipe the drop off your cold nose-end.

In time you have rows of turnips, neatly snagged waiting to be carted off. Carting can be quite a problem if it's wet weather and the land's "clarty". Tractor wheels sink deep and make ruts, you even get wheel-spin and can't make headway at all. So for turnip carting many a farmer turns to his old faithful friend the horse. Horses don't bog down with wheel-spin. They just press their broad, hard feet to the ground, straighten their muscular legs and with a pull which is akin to a lift they simply walk away with a cartload. The land isn't carved up as with a tractor and the poor farmer doesn't get into trouble because of heavy deposits of mud on the highway.

Turnip growing has been a rather contentious subject in latter years. Because they are about eighty per-cent water and because they need such a lot of manual labour many farmers stopped growing them. Instead, they have grown kale. But kale has its disadvantages, too. The biggest being that it has to be cut and carted fresh almost every day. And that can be a most uncomfortable task in wet weather. Other farmers have replaced their turnips and their kale by growing more and better grass and by making silage. But now that we're again developing our system of livestock farming the turnip is winning back some of its former popularity.

You see, turnips, being capable of surviving the rigours of the winter provide good feed for lowland sheep flocks when grass is most scarce. The North country was always noted for what we term "arable flocks" – that is, sheep which eat off the root crops, particularly turnips, especially grown for them. As you travel about the countryside just now you can't help but notice how many more sheep there appear to be and that many are folded on turnip fields, in the natural process of putting fertility into the soil from which will grow organic crops of food.

# 3
## THRESHING WITH JOE

We've had a threshing day. And a grand day it was for the job. Hardly any wind, warm in the bright sunshine, frosty in the shade and dry underfoot.

Joe arrived with his threshing tackle the previous evening and set up for an early start next morning. And when Joe's ready for an early start that means we've got to start much earlier still. You see, Joe hasn't a couple of hours or so of foddering and milking and mucking out byres to do before breakfast. When he arrives on the scene he's ready to start threshing and expects everybody else to be ready too! He doesn't even have to stoke a boiler like when he had a steam engine. All he does nowadays is to press a button to start his tractor.

Now, Joe's been threshing for nigh on sixty years and he's a worker of the old school. Come eight o'clock you can see him standing on top of his threshing machine. As he slips his watch back into his pocket he blows his whistle. His assistant revs up the tractor, the driving belt turns and the thresher drum starts humming. That whistle means "Take Posts" – time is money and the bill has to be paid from eight o'clock. And if everybody doesn't jump to it once Joe's

blown his whistle then he choicely addresses all and sundry from his exalted rostrum on the virtue of promptness and the vice of laziness.

It needs a team of good workers to do a day's threshing, and what we usually do is to help one another as the thresher visits each farm in the neighbourhood – perhaps a day at each place. You see, you've got to have one man, or maybe a couple, on the stack forking sheaves to two chaps on the thresher top who cut the strings and then pass the loose sheaves to Joe who feeds them into the drum. So that's five men on top. You need anther two to bag the grain as it comes pouring out of the chutes – that's at what we call the "money end" of the thresher – that makes seven; and then you need one at the other end forking the bundles, or as we call them "bottles" of straw to another fellow who builds them into a stack. And that makes nine men in all. And if you can get a few more there'll still be work for them because threshing is the one job on the farm where man is slave to the machine. That's because once the thing is started it never eases off, and you've got to keep up with it. If the forker slacks off he gets the benefit of Joe's tongue. If the string cutters slack off – and, by gum, that is a back-aching job because you're stooping all the time – if the string cutters slack off they become overwhelmed with sheaves on their little platform. It's slavish, unrelenting, non-relaxing.

In fact the only respite is if the string should snap on the straw bundler and have to be retied, but that doesn't take long! Or, most welcome break of all, when one of the womenfolk comes out with a basket and shouts "Bait time!" Then, for a few minutes, tea and sandwiches and cakes – what we call our "Ten o'clocks" – and everybody takes the opportunity to dig a hand into the bags of grain to see what sort of a sample has been coming out, to see if the grains are clean, hard, dry and big.

Well, then, after a while, without being noticed Joe has climbed on top again and he blows his whistle; and everybody yells "Hey, thoos off-side!" – but we all gulp the last of our tea and man posts again!

So, hard and pressing as the work is, we do have our bit of fun. For instance, Bill created a bit of a diversion! He was working on the bags. Suddenly he started prancing about shouting "Mouse, Mouse!" Well, there were plenty of cats about and I didn't see why Bill should put on such a feminine performance. So I sort of gaped at him and said "Where?" And he blurted! "It's gone up my trooser leg! It's, it's running round me belly!" Well, it was so funny I couldn't help but laugh even if the grain was pouring over the top of a full bag! He said its feet felt cold; and then that it was "up his back!" I could see it moving under his shirt. I blocked it with my fist; pushing my hand down his shirt neck; pulled it out and threw it to a cat. After that he tied a piece of "John Robert" – that's our name for binder twine – he tied a piece of "John Robert" round the bottom of each trouser leg.

You might think that a combine-harvester which cuts the crop and threshes it in one operation requiring only two men might do away with winter-time threshing days, but it won't. For, one thing, corn in stack is conveniently stored until you need it and it has had the advantage of time to dry naturally in stooks before being stacked. Then grain for seed matures safely in stack and the newly-threshed straw is always fresh, and cattle enjoy a feed of fresh straw as a change from hay.

Yes, even farmers with combines still find it convenient to stack or house some quantity of corn in sheaf and "hev a bit threshing day noo and then", as we say. So we thought, at the time!

# 4
# FIRST FOOT INTO A NEW YEAR

I thought Bill put it feelingly when he came to let the New Year in. "By gum", said he, "it's a grand feeling to know that we've plenty o' good hay to see us through till Spring. Man, I div like to fodder a bite extra to t' beasts on Christmas Day – just because it is Christmas, like – and ken that I won't have to pinch them for it later on. Ay, man alive! I can enjoy me food in comfort then."

Bill has been our "first footer" for many years. When he started he had every qualification for the job – in particular, jet black hair. But it's turned to silver now – what's left of it! I suppose he's typical of first-footers is Bill. Over all those years, whatever the weather, he's always been outside loitering in the lane as the old year ended and the New Year began. And, after the bells have finished ringing and he's felt satisfied that a new year really has started he's come up the yard and knocked on the door. Y'see, he's always made sure of being the first person to whom the door has been opened each year.

And then he's gone through his regular little ceremony. He pulls a log of wood, or a piece of coal, from under his coat and places it on the fire…….. A sign of his wish that the occupants shall have warmth and comfort. Then he shakes hands with everybody and wishes them a Happy New Year. And then, with a mince pie in one hand and a glass of wine in the other he raises them both and says – "All the best!"

We do know – although there's nothing to tell us save past experience – and faith - that in the New Year there'll be a sowing time, a growing time, and a harvest. If there isn't then neither man nor beast will survive through next winter! And those of us who live on the land know, too, that in order to survive we've got to work with Nature, not struggle against her. Y'see, from New Year's Day onwards farmers are constantly looking ahead and planning for the coming Spring. It's the only way. For instance, you've got to be ready to plough as soon as conditions are right – you can't plough when there's frost, or when it's too wet, nor even if it's too dry. And if you do miss the right opportunity then you miss the chance of a crop. So our minds must be alert and our practice in step with Nature's phase.

Although the most severe weather of the winter may still be to come the turn of the year does bring a sense of awareness that Nature has already passed her deepest sleep. You've got to walk across the fields to realise this. In places there's a new greenness over the short sward. And beneath the old turfs of longer grasses you can see tiny darts of green, whilst, in the garden, there's already a life-like look about the buds on the blackcurrant bushes. And, it won't be long until the honeysuckle shows a brave but lonely glint of green in the bare hedgerows. And another thing, we don't now have to lock the hens up quite so soon as we did on those dark days just before Christmas. The days are lengthening! The shortest has passed and we'll never know till this infant year is creeping towards the Summer.

# 5
## A "CLARTY" BUSINESS

There's a good old Northcountry word for describing the wet state of the land. It's "clarty" – that's what it is "clarty"! Wherever you go there's mud. At the field gateways its ankle deep and it sticks to your boots and leggings. And, by gum, you've got to be careful not to trail it into the house and "clart everything up", as they tell us, - otherwise there's a wigging from the womenfolk.

When it's raining the fields squelch as you plod across them and the becks froth and gurgle in spate. "February fill dyke" starts in January. This is the time of year when we can easily check up on the flow of the field drains. If there's a place in a field where the water bubbles up out of the ground, or an odd spot that remains swampy after the rest of the field is reasonably dry, then we know that somewhere round about there a drain is blocked. And then we've got to dig and find it – which is about the "clartiest" job on the farm.

The first thing to do is to look for the outlet into the ditch and then try to figure out if your burst is in a main drain or a branch. Even then you might dig half-a-dozen holes before you strike it. You see, the old drainers didn't leave any plans. Of course, they didn't need any. They had their own systems which they adapted to the contours and, being local men in a profession which passed from father to son, they knew every field drain in the district. But these old-time ditchers are dying out now and it's a lucky farmer who still has one in his parish to refer to for advice, otherwise he's got to scratch about like being on a treasure hunt.

Yes, the old country craftsman who specialised in getting the water off the land with his various trenching spades, scoops and swan-necks, is being replaced by machinery. Every field, y'know, is piped with earthenware draining tiles which are laid end to end at the bottom of a very narrow trench. It's not hard work now like it used to be. The trench is cut with a digging machine fitted to a tractor and filled in again by a tractor fitted with a small bulldozer blade.

Surface water percolates through the broken soil and clay and is led away through the tiles to the ditches. And even the ditches are cleaned out by mechanical scoops nowadays. Spades are out of fashion!

Of course, tile draining is no new thing – it's just the way of doing it that's changed. Many fields were tile drained as far back as a hundred years ago – and there have been various methods of draining for the past two or three hundred years. There was deep draining at about three feet and shallow draining just below the top soil. Deep draining is the practice now because they've got to be far enough down to take the weight of tractors.

One very old method of shallow draining was to plough a deep furrow and lay twigs and brushwood in the bottom and then roll the sod back again. That was one way of draining pools off into the ditches. Then where the clay comes near to the surface another method was to set the field in what we call "lands" or "riggs" when ploughing. You've probably noticed fields like that even today. You can easily pick them out. They're all parallel ridges and furrows. The ridges are called the "lands" or "riggs", and every five or, maybe, eight yards there's a deep furrow. The idea was that the water ran off the "lands" into the furrows and drained away to the ditch on the edge of the field. When they deep-drained so long ago – before they began to manufacture tiles – they laid cobble stones in the trenches and the water seeped away between them.

Well, it would cause some damage if we ploughed the fields into lands and furrows today. Now when we plough we need to make sure that the surface will be level – not all hills and hollows. It would never do, for instance, to bump across humps and hollows with a combine harvester. You would be asking for breakages if you did – and besides you would get such an awful tender place to sit down on!

Land drainage is a serious problem. For one thing it's terribly expensive - costing more than the value of most undrained land. It's a serious problem because most of the old tile drains have been in so long that many of them are perished and choking up – causing the water to bubble up. Really they should be replaced entirely. Sooner or later this will become a big national problem. But for the time being we've got to patch them here and there as best we can. It is a job that the specialist drainer would have done in the summer but the farmer is too busy with other things then and so it becomes his lot to tackle it in Winter – when the land is "clarty".

# 6
## MOVING AT CANDLEMAS

Candlemas Day – February the Second. In Scotland and the English Border country it's the first Quarter Day and it's the day upon which farm rents fall due. Most other English farms are what we term "Lady Day" places, meaning that the year's rent falls due on March 25th. Usually the rent is paid half-yearly on Candlemas farms and the first half-yearly instalment is paid on Lammas Day; that is, on August the first which, in the Church's Calendar, is the festival of the wheat harvest.

Candlemas is a Christian festival commemorating in the Roman Catholic Church the Purification of the Virgin Mary and in the Eastern Churches the Presentation of Christ in the Temple. The Anglican prayer book, however, retains both these commemorations and the name "Candlemas" dates from the eleventh century, when the ceremony of blessing the candles and carrying them in procession began.

For the farmer Candlemas Day is the start of a new farming year. It's the anniversary of the day upon which he became the occupier and it's the day upon which he'll end his tenancy should he retire or take over another place.

At one time from about November onwards there used to be a large number of farm sales – lock, stock and barrel. It was then the custom, when a farmer decided to change his farm, for him to sell all his crop, implements and livestock at a sale arranged on the farm. Under that system he did, of course, still remain the occupier of the now unstocked farm until the Second of February but, meantime, he has to find another farm. This, incidentally, was a much easier proposition then than it is nowadays.

Having finally got a farm to his liking, he set about attending one farm sale after anther buying in livestock, crop and implements with which to stock and equip the new place. The only thing he didn't need to buy was muck because there's a law of good husbandry that farm-yard manure produced on the farm must not be sold off – or, at least, not more than a certain limited amount.

When the great day of removal came – Candlemas Day – he'd load all his furniture, goods and chattels and move in to the new farm as the old occupier moved out. For so many complete farm changes to take place in a single day was really a wonderful operation. It was made possible by all the neighbouring farmers and their staffs turning up to help with the loading, transport and unloading. By nightfall the complete changes had been made and the new occupiers settled in on their respective farms.

During the period of waiting for Candlemas when, as you can see, there could be no real farming activity there was often little progress with any ploughing. So a new occupier was, as a rule, faced with a back log of ploughing to be made up. And this was where good neighbourliness came to the rescue. It was the tradition for all neighbouring farmers to give the new occupier the benefit of a Ploughing Day. By arrangement they'd each take a team of horses and a plough on an agreed day and all set to work ploughing for the new neighbour. There may have been a dozen or more ploughs. And, in this way they brought the farm programme up to date so that the new man didn't start the Spring at a disadvantage.

Well, of course, Candlemas farm changes are still the rule – except for Lady Day places – but, nowadays instead of having a sale it's the practice to move everything from the old farm to the new one. And, really, this is much more sensible. However, this change has come about for good reason. For one thing vacant farms are so rare nowadays that it isn't very safe to give notice to leave one until you're reasonably sure of getting another. Also, another aspect is that most herds of cattle nowadays are carefully bred usually pedigreed – they're TB free and represent a strain which the farmer has built up into a herd over many years. So naturally, he doesn't wish to part with them except if he decides to retire and have a displenishing sale. Besides, it seems a bit daft to sell everything, machinery and all, only to have to spend a lot more money replacing it all. So that's why nowadays you sometimes hear of a modern Noah's Ark operation in which a farmer engages a railway train or a fleet or trucks to move him and his belongings.

Candlemas is an important date for all farmers apart from being Rent Day or Moving Day. It's a reckoning time, for there's an old dictum that if there's still half the fodder crop to eat at February the Second then there should be enough to last until the grass grows in the Spring.

# 7

# THE FUR-COATED UNDERGROUND ENGINEER

# – THE MOLE

In my part of the country we call him the "mowdie", and the little hillocks of soil he pushes up in the fields we call "mowdie-warps". As soon as the hard frost ends there comes a sudden rash of these earthy "pimples" over many a green field.

These molehills are a nuisance. For one thing, taking them all together, they reduce the grazing area and, for another, they make a field so rough that they break mowing knives as they bump and clatter over them. Apart from the hillocks, however, moles aren't really any bother to the farmer. They don't eat crops – their diet is worms and earth insects. Some folk even reckon that a few moles are worth encouraging because their tunnels assist surface drainage. Well, that's as it may be, but "mowdies" are pretty good at making tunnels in which they are not going to be drowned!

Of course, they are fairly active all the year round but they get extra busy following a hard frost. That's understandable considering that the land has been iron hard. But, even so, a "mowdie" is a defiant little fellow and it takes a very severe frost to stop him finding some place where he can break through the crust of frozen earth to heave out his surplus soil. He shoves up a ragged pattern of dark blots on the snow, too. And when the earth is free again he's working overtime.

It's only on rare occasions that you ever see a mole – although he's not a rare animal – except on the Isle of Man and in Ireland where he doesn't exist at all! Robbie Burns would say "he's a tim'rous beastie". If you stand still and quiet among his latest earthworks you might find a heap of soil being pushed up at your feet. You might see a small red, pig-like snout peep out as the crumbly soil cascades into an ever-growing mound. Beside a stream you may even be lucky enough to see his clean, black velvety body scuffle out of his gallery as he goes to drink. But just make a single move and at once the excavation stops. Or, if he's out on the surface, he simply "melts" back into the earth – so rapidly does he burrow.

Sometimes you can dig him out with a spade – if you're as quick as lightening! Mind you, you've got to be standing there ready poised at the spot where he starts to work! Then a sudden thrust of the spade, an upward flick and – if you're lucky – he rolls out on to the grass in a spray of soil. Leap after him now and grab him quick, because he'll tunnel himself under again in a twinkling!

Whilst it's necessary to get rid of moles because they become such a pest you need to employ surer methods than this one, of course. However, I once had a sheepdog which was a dab hand at catching moles. After waiting patiently for the right moment she would pounce on the earth and in the same swift movement fling the "gentleman in black" up in the air!

Years ago almost every parish had its professional mole-catcher. Farmers used to pay him an annual service fee of something like three-pence an acre. He would cure the skins of his catches and sell them to the furriers. The carcasses he hung on the fence of each field in order that the farmer saw the measure of his success. But he never completely rid the land of moles. It was always said that he left a couple on each farm to breed from! He was careful not to work himself out of business.

Apart from the off-chance catch by a dog or using a spade when a "mowdie" is actually pushing up a hillock, the place to trap moles is not among the molehills. You see, those mounds of earth are at the end of branch tunnels. The main runs along which the moles pass to and fro have no hillocks on them. The sides of a main run are tightly compressed as though the mole has bored his way through the soil and at the same time packed the sides with his strong human-like hands. In fact, so strong is the mole that it has been estimated he can overcome a force the equivalent of thirty times his own weight! Molehills, it seems, are mostly of the pulverised soil which has been scratched through in search of food and then each heap pushed up through a special shaft to get it out of the way.

The art of mole-catching, for which traps were used, is possessed by few folk nowadays. The professional mole catcher has gone – or, at least, is a very rare person. The farmer has called in the chemist. Nowadays it is Ministry of Agriculture men called Pest Officers with motor cars and brief cases, who do the job or, at any rate, show the farmer how to do it – and they use poison!

# 8
## BILLY THE BULL

*Rosie*

Rosie was a Red Shorthorn. She was an in-calf heifer when father bought her. I was just a school-lad at the time and I well remember the dark winter evening when a cattle wagon brought her. It was that cloudy sort of weather when the wind blows soft. When it's warm enough to leave the top half of the byre door open; when the lanes and gateways are muddy; the sort of weather when Tom remarks to Dick "Not a bad sort of a neet," and Dick replies, "No, not so bad, but it could easy rain". Just the sort of weather you'd call "catchy" if you were expecting the threshing machine.

The inside of a byre full of cows smells good on such a night and the all-embracing warmth as you step inside is one of the most comfortable feelings you can experience. Nearly all the other cows were lying down content and full, chewing their cud, as Rosie was led to the stall which was to be hers for more years than any of us ever guessed. I can remember a group of us – the family and one or two others – standing in the byre that night examining Rosie by the light of a stable lantern. We had no electricity in those days.

Well, we handled her all over and remarked on almost every part of her anatomy. "A nice fettle," said Bill, grasping a horny handful of beef over her ribs – "and fit," he added, as he pulled her loose healthy skin as if it was elastic. Then he slid his hand between her buttocks and stretched the smooth, silky skin of her udder. "Aye, she's a reet un," he said, "plenty o' room for milk there." Then he said, "Aye" again as though emphasising his contemplation and, after a long pause, "Aye ... aye ... aye, she'll have a grand bag when she's due, and it'll have a teat on each corner." To which everyone replied in ragged unison – "Aye". And I knew that they could pay no better compliment to any dairy cow.

For the next half hour or so Rosie was for me a practical object lesson. My father instructed me in her points. And, one after the other, the menfolk interjected appropriate remarks – in their countrymen's way – which fixed the information in my mind for all time; far more effectively than any text book could have done. To sum up, she was what they described as a "milky sort". Oh, yes, she would be a good milker all right. The final qualification was that she'd a nice face – the last part we'd looked at really closely! She was, as Tom put it "dairy lookin' – a good length between eye and nose." Funny isn't it, to think that if Rosie had been human we'd have gained our impression, good or bad, from her face first of all! But, y'know, many a time after that we did credit Rosie with being human – well, almost human. And I can tell you this – that Rosie and my dog Bell and a few others taught me to recognize facial expressions in animals. Believe me, they all have personalities and temperaments of one degree or another.

Rosie was a placid, determined kind. She was an individualist and she was peace itself. Many another cow I've been glad to get rid of in its time, but never Rosie. Well, she wasn't long in settling in to her new home. In due time her first calf was born and the quality of rich milk she yielded fulfilled the promise of all her physical signs. In fact, Rosie proved to be too good to part with. Other cows joined the herd and other cows left the herd – some bought-in, some home-bred, but Rosie stayed on for ever. She became part of the premises, as you might say – no other cow ever stood in her stall – and she became a tradition. She was a five-gallon-milker and extraordinary butter-producer. She would be about twenty-two years old when she died and during her life-time she had given birth to no fewer than sixteen calves ten heifers and six bulls – all of which lived. And, in addition she had produced almost a hundred times her own weight in milk!

Now, it's about one of Rosie's offspring that I want to tell you. We called him "Billy" – Billy the Bull. But, first, let me finish telling you a little more about the old girl herself. She was, as I told you before, almost human. If the field gates were open she would come home at milking-time without being called; and after milking she would stroll quietly back to the meadow again. She was queen of the herd right enough and always took her place in front of the column each time the herd came up – or went down – the lane. And woe-betide any other cow which tried to march out in front. Rosie would give it a poke in the ribs with her horns by way of explaining that its place was to the rear – only the queen walks in front.

And, by the way, those horns of hers are worth mentioning. In her youth they

*Billy*

were perfectly shaped both alike and correctly balanced. But as she grew older (and, like all horned cows, with the birth of each calf a ringed ridge grew on each horn) they curved downwards and inwards until the points were touching her eyelids and we had to saw the end off each one to prevent them growing into her eyes.

Well, now about Billy. Billy was Rosie's last calf her sixteenth. She had given birth to a run of bulls for two or three years and we were hoping she would leave us a heifer this time with which to carry on her strain. But whatever she left us, this was to be the last calf she would have. We would milk her during lactation and then she could go into honourable retirement. There was to be no slaughter-house for Rosie – she was one of the family, everybody's pet; and, y'know, she had helped to rear a couple of hefty lads, for my brother and I had supped her milk – gallons and gallons of it – almost exclusively.

It was the back-end of the year when Billy was calved. Somewhat similar weather to when Rosie came as a heifer eighteen odd years earlier. He arrived unassisted during the night and was lying in the straw when I went into the byre with a stable lamp about six o'clock that dark winter's morning. A chubby, roan haired little fellow he was, with dumpy nose and a broad back. I picked him up and popped him into a bed of deep straw in a calf-pen. Rosie was lying down and Billy didn't look as though he'd had a 'draw' at the 'pantry'. Y'see, he obviously hadn't been long born; mind you, he was dry so perhaps he had arrived about three o'clock or so – time enough to have his first suckle, of course. But his mouth and nostrils were just a wee bit cold, and if he had suckled I would have expected him to be glowing with warmth and perhaps have a few frothy bubbles still clinging to his whiskers.

Anyhow, things seemed a bit odd to me. I decided to give him a feed of Rosie's new milk right away – the first milking we call the "beastings"; it's thick, yellow and extra rich. And I would give Rosie a drink of water with the chill taken off, and a warm bran mash. Alas, however Rosie was down and she couldn't get up.

I struggled with her trying to ease her to her feet. But it was no use. She became helpless. Even her will to stand had gone. And when a cow gets to that state it is just a great ungainly heap of beef and opposes all your efforts. It's just a dead-weight that cannot be man-handled.

The only thing for me to do was to give her the drink and the mash – which she took readily enough – try to squeeze some milk from her and call the vet. Billy, of course, had to be fed with milk from another cow.

Well, the trouble turned out to be a form of paralysis. We rigged a sling and hoisted her to her feet for periods of an hour or two at a time but she still failed to stand. Despite all the doctoring she gradually grew weaker, lost her appetite, and one night passed quietly away. Next morning we hauled her body out of the stall she had occupied for such a long time, and I can tell you it wasn't without some heart-ache, as you can understand, that we loaded her on the truck for the knackery. That was the end of faithful Rosie, and Billy, being her last-born, came in for far more attention than he would have otherwise enjoyed. He supped lashings of milk and was fed on plenty of the best of everything. By gum, did he thrive! When summer came he ran loose in the calf paddock and, quite frankly, everybody made a pet of him – too much of a pet as I was to learn to my cost later. If you found time to sit in the paddock on a warm summer evening Billy would come sniffing round you and hold his head out whilst you scratched his nose. Then he would lie down beside you and lay his great heavy head across your lap because he liked to have his chin and neck stroked! Oh, yes, he was really quite ridiculously spoiled!

Well, there's a time comes when these animals get just too big and a bit too playful to be regarded as pets any more. And Billy was no exception. In fact he was extra big and could be extra playful. Even so, unwisely, he was never regarded as dangerous. Although one old countrywoman described having watched him rampaging round the field as though he was – as she quite seriously put it – "The varra devil his sell". Because, y'know, all bulls should be regarded as dangerous however quiet or friendly they may appear to be.

Now, Billy developed into a really handsome young bull and became the consort of a bevy of selected shorthorn heifers. Then one day he blotted his copy book. His friendliness towards human beings was a bygone. And it was I who was to be brought to the full and painful realization of that fact.

On this particular day when I went to the field where Billy and his heifers were pastured I found him standing across the gateway barring my entrance. I couldn't open the gate for him. "Come on, Billy, lad, get on," I commanded, but he stood stubbornly rooted. So I reached over and gave him a hearty slap with a flat hand, eased the gate open, and squeezed through. And as I got through I said, "Come, my old lad, move on!" But he was in no mind to co-operate. He just fixed me with a pair of wicked eyes. Then with the suddenness of a rocket he sprang forward and butted me – slam! – in the pit of my stomach. Well, I fell over backwards into a pool of mud and water and as soon as I scrambled to my feet he dumped me from there into a holly bush. He'd got me cornered and he knew it. So did I! He came at me again and rolled me into the mud once more and this time tried to kneel on me. Now we were desperate. It was an out-and-out fight between us. I knew that if he got his knees on me he would pin me down until he had gored me to death! His horns were fortunately short but they had already made my ribs sting and I wasn't for having any more punishment. I wriggled away as he came down on his knees and threw my arms around his thick neck. He tossed his head and I hung on, dangling over his face like a mask. Each time my feet were on the ground I tried to push his head away from my middle. I pushed with all my might. I never knew I was so strong – perhaps it was thanks to Rosie's rich milk! My chance came when he eased back for a fresh attack and I slid to the side of his neck – still hanging on with both arms and keeping close in to him. Billy wasn't getting all his own way now. It was as though he had a leech on his neck and he couldn't shake me off. But, believe me, I certainly wasn't for staying there any longer than was necessary.

At last his first mad spasm seemed to have abated. He started running backwards in his efforts to shake me loose and all the time I was looking for a way of escape before spasm number two overcame him. My eyes were scanning the fence. I must get over that fence as soon as ever I dare leave go. Six wide strides away was the fence and safety. I gave Billy one final super strong push, flung myself clear and leapt that fence as though I'd got springs in my heels.

Now Billy was thwarted. He pawed at the grass and flung scoops of turf into the air. And there I left him snorting and bellowing his bad temper. I limped home – battered and bruised, aching and sore, tattered and muddy – thankful to be still in one piece. But Billy had shot his bolt. Now the butcher would shoot a bolt into him. His immediate future was changed from being a stock-bull to becoming some of the roast beef of old England. Certainly a premature but, perhaps, not an entirely inglorious end. But, y'know if Rosie's last calf had been a heifer – but then there wouldn't have been this tale to tell, would there?

# 9

# MORE GLUTTENS AND FEWER FRIENDS

Perhaps you've sometimes wondered what it feels like to be ploughing a field surrounded by a flock of seagulls. Well, seagulls and ploughing are most fascinating and picturesque when the ploughman is working with a team of horses. It's good to have the feel of the plough in your hands, the tang of the soil in your nostrils and the screeching chatter of the seagulls in your ears. But that's all spoiled nowadays with the roar and smell of the tractor engine. Also, with the horse plough we ploughed a single furrow at a time and the seagulls fed leisurely and cleared up almost every earthworm and wireworm to be found in each furrow as it was drawn. With a tractor we plough two and three furrows at a time and worm-hunting is much more of a scramble. In fact, there's little chance of the gulls getting anything out of any but the last furrow – and even then they've got to be quick.

Well, after the ploughing and the cultivating – that is, when we've got a seed-bed made – it's the turn of the black and the grey marauders to fill their bellies. As soon as we bring out the bags of seed-corn, down come the crows, rooks, jackdaws and pigeons. They're not so friendly and they keep their distance – they're after devouring the grain as soon as we've sown it.

It's always reckoned a good idea to sow an extra bag of corn "just for the crows" because if you sow only the correct seeding rate the crop will be thinner than it should be when the crows have claimed their share. Sometimes a whole field has to be resown after the crows and pigeons have been on it. They're cunning blighters too. They seem to know exactly how far a gun will fire and they know whether or not you're carrying a gun. Go into a field without one and they'll dibble away with their beaks quite cheekily. But have a gun in your hand – try hiding it behind your back, if you like – and they'll be off. They'll never let you get near to them. You've got to use really clever tactics to outwit a crow. They even get wise to the most life-like scarecrows in time.

There is one valuable and friendly bird which is really a watch-dog against crows and that is the peewit or plover – also known as the landrail. Peewits, especially when nesting, get really angry when crows come on the scene. They immediately go up to challenge them. That's about the only time that a crow flies fast – when a peewit stoops and swirls round it in a bewildering display of aerobatics.

Unfortunately, the population of peewits has declined as rapidly as that of crows and pigeons has increased. This is a great pity because the peewit – or plover – is one of our most useful birds. It does no damage to crops but lives on a variety of harmful insects. I'm afraid we have to blame motorized farming for its disappearance.

Y'see, peewits nest on the ground – actually out in the open on arable fields. Nesting time coincides with about the end of sowing time and they usually nest among the crumbly clods of a newly-sown corn field. The nests, comprising a few wisps of grass, and the eggs – they lay only four – are not easy to see against the soil. However, when the field was rolled by a horse pulling a seven or eight foot wide roller, the chap leading the horse had a chance to find these nests. And when he did so he would guide his roller carefully round them so as not to break the eggs. Nowadays, a tractor pulls as many as three rollers at a time – probably a total width of twenty-four feet, and the driver hasn't a chance to see what's on the ground and, consequently, a whole generation of peewits throughout the country is wiped out each spring. No wonder, then, that there are so few.

There doesn't seem to be much we can do about this – I suppose they are sacrificed in the name of progress. But I do think if we could only hear more "peewit, peewit", we'd hear less "caw, caw".

# 10

## STYLISH FURROWS

*Nelson Tamblin - Champion Ploughman*

There's seldom a week passes during the winter without a ploughing match being held somewhere – weather permitting. And it's surprising what a big number of ploughing matches are held despite frost, snow, rain, gales, fogs and floods.

Now ploughing is the first operation in cultivating the land, and the plough is the key which unlocks the fertility of the earth. If ploughmen around the globe missed the opportunity to plough we'd all starve to death in a matter of twelve months. And if land isn't ploughed properly then the crops cannot be as good as they should be. For instance, it's very necessary that every bit of ground, when ploughing, should be turned over otherwise the weeds will flourish.

Now, what is good ploughing? How do we judge it? Well, there are various styles of the ploughman's art. Style often varies from locality to locality according to the structure and depth of the soil, normal climatic condition and, also, according to the purpose for which the land is being ploughed – that is, according to the requirements of the crop to be planted; although that isn't quite so important nowadays as it used to be before the introduction of machines which, after ploughing, work the soil into a tilth suitable for almost any crop.

There are two basic styles of ploughing – the old fashioned oat seed furrow and the modern general purpose furrow.

Oat seed furrow is also known as high cut or high crested work because of its pointed shape, and it's as near to ploughing perfection as skill can achieve. You can only see this high cut furrow at ploughing matches nowadays – except, perhaps, in some places where the land is a stiff clay and the climate wet. Then you see, it's better to cut the soil so that it stands up fairly high, so that it dries out quicker and breaks up more easily than if the furrow slice is nearly flat. High cut ploughing was the style used when grain was sown by hand – that's why it was called Oat Seed Furrow. The oats were sown direct on to the ploughing. Therefore, the slices had to be narrow so as not to leave too wide a space between the rows of grain. They had to be tightly packed together – so that there could be no space through which the grain could slip and be lost under the sod; the crest of the upturned sod had to be high so that, after the corn was sown, all that was needed was a stroke of the spike harrows to break the soil down into a covering tilth. Also, the sward had to be completely buried so that grass and weeds wouldn't grow in competition with the crop. To ensure this tight packing the furrows had to be all the same size, even and dead straight. In fact, expert ploughmen insist that they shouldn't vary from one end of the field to the other, and each from each, by as much as the breadth of a penny! And if you are to take a look at a cross-section of the furrows they should all appear as equilateral triangles of similar dimensions. In fact, they should be so much alike that you should have to count them and divide by two to find out where the ploughing was begun in the middle of the plot! And, although it may be

unnecessary to plough that style generally nowadays, it does still remain the one type of ploughing which has a single specific purpose – that is for the hand-sowing of corn. And there can be no argument about it – it's either done well or it isn't. Even a non-ploughman can see that.

Now, general purpose ploughing is a very loose term indeed. Tom, Dick and Harry may all plough the same style of work but each has a different purpose in mind – and it's done with a plough that turns a broad, almost flat slice. It may be deep ploughing for potatoes and roots or it may be shallow for grain or because the soil is thin. But whatever the crop the soil will later be chopped into a tilth with a series of implements such as the "oat-seed-furrow man" never possessed. He only used a plough, a set of harrows and a roller.

Unfortunately, today's implements are also capable of making bad ploughing look good without removing the faults – they just cover them up. If all the ground isn't turned over the weeds grow just the same. If the ridge, where the ploughing was begun is too high, or if the last furrow where the ploughing finished is too deep, then there is a risk of damage to harvest machines and wagons which have to bump over an uneven surface.

The purpose of ploughing matches is to encourage and maintain the high degree of skill which is necessary to achieve the best benefits of good cultivation. Y'see, anyone can drive a tractor – that's not difficult – but it does take a better man to plough with one. The secret lies in understanding one's plough and the soil and in having some mathematical ingenuity.

A good ploughman is one who understands perfectly the adjustment of his plough. It's all in precision setting of the share which cuts the sod horizontally, of the coulter which cuts it vertically and of the mouldboard which turns it over. When that's done correctly a ploughed field is a work of art and a pleasure to look upon and is the first step towards a good crop.

*Tractor ploughing match*

*"Rigg and furrow" near Uldale*

# 11
## THE GOOD OLD PLOUGH

There's nothing more joyfully satisfying in a solid, quiet sort of way than to lean on the gate you've just closed and look back over the field you've just sown and rolled flat and finished with. That is, finished with until you take the binder or the combine in at harvest-time. You stand there and recall that not many weeks ago that field was waterlogged and you had no idea as to when you'd be able to plough it! Now, at long last, it's just a piece of neatly rolled soil. There's nothing more you can do with it. You've done all that man can do. You believe the seeds you've sown will grow and you expect the shoots to appear in about a fortnight's time.

Now, every time I've sown a field of corn or planted potatoes or any other crop I've always looked back across it when I've finished and I've never escaped the rather frightening thought – "Wouldn't it be awful if it stayed like that and nothing grew!" And y'know, if nothing does grow on the fields that are soil-side-up – well, there'll be nothing to eat! - and, we won't live to see another spring!

And that brings me to the very essence of farming the land. It is not, as some people suggest, "a battle with Nature". The fact is you can't grow food unless you co-operate with Nature. And it's upon that truth that the fundamental tillage of the soil is based. And the basic tool with which man does his part of the co-operation is the plough. Because, you see, the plough is really the key with which we unlock the earth's fertility.

Well, there's a lot in this business of ploughing. It's a craftsman's job and, done properly, it's a work of art. There's much more to it than ploughing a straight furrow. In fact, under some conditions, the ploughman doesn't plough straight but follows the contours. The main feature is to produce soil for a seed-bed and, in doing that, to make sure of turning in all the grass and other top growth so that it won't grow in competition with the new crop. Also, you've got to avoid making hills and hollows where the ploughing starts and finishes.

Now this seed-bed is all-important because it has to be pure, weed-free soil on top of an upturned sod which is packed against the next upturned sod tight enough to prevent any grain slipping underneath where it wouldn't get a chance to grow. It's not really easy to define a "seed-bed" but I heard a ploughman describe one picturesquely when he said that "a bed consists of two parts, first, a clean, cosy place to lie on and, second, a good covering". What he meant was clean, free soil with the grass out of sight, for the seed to lie on and, a good "tilth", a free soil with which to cover the seed. You get the tilth by using the harrows on the ploughing.

No matter what crop you wish to grow, whether it be corn, potatoes, roots, or grass for hay or grazing, you can't establish a crop at all until you've dug up some soil and prepared it into a tilth of a texture which best suits the kind of seed to be planted. Of course, to help the land maintain its fertility year after year it is necessary to add manure and fertilisers. It all demands a lot of careful study. A study of each individual field, of your particular climate, of crop characteristics and so on.

So, having worked with Nature in this way, you know as you look back over the field of your labours that Nature will do the rest. You've put the seed to bed when Nature is wakening up! And you know, too, that the vital tool which for more than two-thousand years has made it possible for man to work with Nature in order to grow food is none other than the good old plough.

*Horse plough - wooden stilts*

*Modern horse plough*

*Semi-digger stubble ploughing*

# 12

## HAYMAKING THEN AND NOW

The plough is laid up and the mowing machine has been hauled from the implement shed - it will be haytime suddenly. One day you see the first field of new mown grass and then, as you journey on through the countryside, there are surprisingly many more of them. It is as though the season has suddenly bounced from spring to summer.

But, we don't hear the chatter of the mowing machines like we used to do. The roar of the tractors drowns it. When horses provided the power it was usual for the chattering knives and the sharp staccato clicks of the cog wheels, as the corners were turned, to echo across the fields as early as sun-rise. We were out at dawn with the horses and "took over", as it were, from the Dawn Chorus. The idea was to mow as much as possible before breakfast and then again after supper – before and after the heat of the day. That was out of consideration for the horses because a mowing machine is a heavy draught. And, if you've never worked in the open air at that time of morning then you've never experienced the best part of the day.

But the tractor doesn't require that kind of consideration. It roars away regardless of heat or flies and is only stopped when the driver needs a break, or a knife needs sharpening. And, I'm afraid, because the tractor shows no feeling the knives are certainly not sharpened or the machinery oiled as often as they used to be.

The farmer used to lay in a new stock of wooden hay rakes and pitch forks and arrange for extra hands to help with the hay harvest. Without a rake or a pitchfork a person was useless in a hayfield. First the swathes – that's the name for the rows of grass cut by the mower – the swathes had to be turned over and, until the farmer became equipped with a horse-drawn mechanized turner, it took a lot of men and women to do the job using handrakes. The more the better. If you were by yourself, once round a big field with a handrake nearly broke your heart when you saw how much there was still to do!

Then when the crop was dry enough there was the task of raking it into thick windrows and building it into cocks or maybe big pikes. And after that there came the carting and the stacking and then the raking clean of the field – a job which women often did. However, the sequence of haytime operations is seldom as straight forward as that. In tricky weather you might turn the hay and cock it and shake it out and cock it again many times before it was fit to house. Of course, it is long since hand-work was the vogue. There was a lot of excellent horse machinery which made comparatively light of haymaking since those days.

With the introduction of the tractor, horse machinery was adapted and is now designed specially for the tractor. The farmer doesn't find it necessary any longer to lay in a big stock of rakes and forks. There aren't enough hands to use them if he did. Instead he can just about make haytime a one-man operation and never touch either fork or rake.

Haytime is made really easy now. A chap rides round a field driving a tractor mower. When the swaths are ready to turn he rides round again towing a turner. And as soon as the hay is quite dry he rides round again pulling a pick-up baler which lifts the hay cleanly off the ground and ties it into neat bales – each weighing about four stone. A couple of fellows can load and cart them to the barn. In place of using the old pitchfork one of them now puts the bales on to a mobile elevator at ground level and the other takes them off as they arrive at the top and neatly stacks them.

So, as you can see, there's very little manhandling nowadays. Of course, it takes time and it takes money to get all the necessary tackle – and then when you have got it you still need – yes, you do — you still need the favour of the weather!

*Mowing grass*

*Hay Pike*

# 13
## THE BORDER COLLIE

Long ago professional drovers used to drive sheep from Scotland and the North of England to London's Smithfield Market. It must have been a tough job in those days of no roads! I believe the staple diet of men and dogs on their slow overland treks was a supply of oat-meal, carried in a leathern bag, and water from the mountain streams and springs. The sheep, of course, lived by grazing on the way. The dogs were important as guards as well as for herding. Local history tells us that many a robbers' raid carried off a goodly flock over Dunmail Raise!

Perhaps it was the drovers who developed the technique of training dogs to obey signals, such as whistled commands to direct them to go right and left and so drive the sheep in desired directions. And, perhaps, when they returned from Smithfield to the hills of Scotland and the North for more sheep they might have sold some of their trained dogs to the hill-men. If this is what happened it's not difficult to understand that dogs so trained would enable the crofters to enlarge their modest flocks. Y'see, they would be able to turn sheep to graze on the open mountains and could be sure of collecting them all together again. That is more than can be done without the help of dogs. No man can be sufficiently fleet of foot to run up crags in an attempt to round up agile sheep! More sheep on the hills meant more business for the Smithfield drovers, too!

The capabilities of these dogs made it possible to embark on sheep-ranching; the hill-men soon realized they could develop the aptitude of the dogs to serve them well.

Generations of breeding from the fittest specimen, which also displayed a lively instinct for the work, has resulted in that super-intelligent canine – the Border Collie. Now if you ask me what breed of dog I consider to be of the greatest service to man I would say "the Sheepdog". Indirectly the sheepdog serves us all. We all wear wool and most of us like a bit of mutton! The sheepdog takes care of both! "There's no good flock without a good shepherd, and there's no good shepherd without a good dog".

Throughout the years shepherds have learnt, and are learning, just as much from the dogs they train as do the dogs themselves. Each had its own peculiar style of working. It's no use the shepherd trying to decide what the style of his dog should be. He's got to study and understand the natural style of his dog. Some of the world's most experienced authorities on the training of sheepdogs have told me the same thing. The best way to get genuine co-operation from these remarkably intelligent canines is to allow the dogs to use their own initiative. Training consists almost entirely of teaching them to know what they are doing, to be self-reliant, self-confident, and to work with their master. All these 'handlers' carefully avoid ever training a dog to respond to commands in mechanical fashion.

You must not get the impression that a Border Collie responds to a series of signals as would some radio-controlled robot, automatically starting and stopping at the touch of a button. If this thought should put ideas into the mind of some inventive genius let me hasten to assure you that no "doodle-dog" device would ever replace a sheepdog!

A good sheepdog when at work driving sheep on the road is more liable to be run over by a car than a less conscientious dog, because it will not concern itself with anything but its task. A less conscientious dog looks after itself and leaves its charges to work out their own salvation. So, motorist, should you at any time on your travels be confronted by a flock of sheep and some sheepdogs, please don't become impatient if a sheepdog completely ignores you and settles itself in the middle of the road in front of your car. Instead, just slow down and admire that faithful heart, loyally doing its duty even at the risk of being killed by your machine.

This determination by a sheepdog to stand its ground whatever the odds is called "force" or "eye". You usually get a good display of "force" when a dog is faced by a stubborn ewe. Very often a stubborn ewe, and always when it has lambs, will face up to the dog, angrily stamp its front feet, and even butt! When a dog holds its ground despite these threats, fixes its gaze on the eyes of the sheep, and even slowly advances an inch or two at a time until its will-power dominates that of the sheep, we say it has "a good eye" or "plenty of force".

A good "eye" denotes determination coupled with patience. Essential for a sheepdog which has to herd sheep among dangerous crags, for instance. A rough, unsteady dog would be too rash and would scare the sheep. It must have courage to deal with stubborn sheep, be patient and not vicious. These qualities are an assurance that it will not bark, snap, become excited and frighten sheep or rush them unduly. This is particularly important when herding in-lamb ewes or manoeuvring over-adventurous and wayward sheep from some dangerous precipice where a slip may end in a death crash over the crags. In such situations a dog must be capable of thinking for itself and using its own initiative, for it may be working out of sight of its master.

Some years ago, Bright, a dog of Mr Joseph Relph's, found three sheep in a very awkward position on Wanthwaite Crags. He was working on his own out of his master's sight and it was later established that before he succeeded in driving those sheep to safety he had struggled hard and patiently for five hours. Towards dusk he arrived with them safely in the farm yard, wagging his tail and obviously happy that his patience and perseverance had triumphed.

Perhaps the best example of "force" was displayed by Spy, champion of Ireland, owned by Mr Lionel Pennefather. At a trials Spy was beset by a particularly stubborn sheep which stood its ground firmly, stamped a foot and made as if to butt its warden. But Spy just fixed his eyes on those of the sheep and advanced quietly and determinedly, a little at a time nearer and nearer to his obstinate ward.

The crowd was tense with excitement and wondered whose will-power would prevail - the sheep's or the dog's. Still unperturbed Spy advanced until he was right up to the sheep, face to face, and then he gently reached forward and licked the sheep's nose! This was too much for the bewildered sheep and she turned tail and trotted off to rejoin her mates.

Sheepdogs are born with an instinct to gather and herd, and it is a delight to watch Border Collie puppies mischief-bound in the farmyard. They will ever so gently creep round the poultry and roguishly manoeuvre them into a corner. Eventually the hens become used to this little game and decide to ignore the puppies and go on scratching and picking in the normal way. The pups know by instinct that they must not yap or snap and when ignored by hens, when they are wanting fun, they will take a mischievous little jump on all fours and so cause a flutter in order to get the hens to move.

When snow is thick on the mountains fell dogs are adept at finding sheep that are snow bound. A dog called Floss was extremely good at this work and once in Whitbeck Ghyll on Skiddaw she "marked" in the snow drift. The shepherds dug in and found a number of buried sheep, but although they got them safely out Floss "marked" again at the bottom of the hole, and as she persisted in this they dug deeper and discovered yet another sheep which had been snowbound beneath the first lot. Although the scent of the first lot must have still remained in the hole Floss was quite confident that there was still another farther down.

This same dog once marked a big drift and although shepherds dug all round and prodded deep into the snow with their long crooks they could not find anything and went on.

Some seven weeks later passing that way again Floss once more "marked" at the same spot. The snow had settled considerably by now and on digging again they found a sheep. It had eaten what moss and grass it could find in its snow chamber, which the heat of its body had thawed around it, and then eaten of its own wool. It was almost a skeleton but careful nursing brought it back to health again and it became known as "Snowy".

Fortunately, the snow does not usually stay long in most parts of Cumberland, thanks to our nearness to the sea and mild effects of the Gulf Stream Drift.

The longest spell of snow in recent years occurred in 1947 and lasted seven weeks. The death toll among the fell flocks was extremely heavy. It meant big losses to farmers but was probably to their benefit in the long run because at that time shepherds were concerned about the fells becoming overstocked with sheep to such an extent that sheep diseases were on the increase.

Perhaps the severity of that particular winter was Nature's way of making up the balance. So many sheep perished that flock numbers were reduced and the fellsides and valley fields, being locked under a carpet of snow, had seven weeks respite from being wandered over and grazed.

This enforced "resting" period undoubtedly restricted the spread of some ailments just like it is possible to eliminate the footrot germ from a pasture by keeping sheep off it for a matter of a couple of weeks.

In Ireland, Mr Lionel Pennefather tried an experiment, using ducks and a miniature course instead of sheep. Of course, sheepdogs are often used of an evening by the farmer's wife when she wants to pen the ducks up for the night. But his idea was to demonstrate the trust which could be placed in a properly trained dog in regard to its associations with the feathered world, and as a result of this, for the very first time in public, duck-herding was presented at the trials held at Workington.

During the making of the film, "Sheepdog of the Hills," we were for some time billeted on a farm in Devon. One evening Moss was lying in the orchard when our hostess went there to pen up her chickens for the night. Seeing that she was having some difficulty old Moss voluntarily went over and very gently and coaxingly helped her to guide them into the coop. Each night after that wherever Moss was about the farm or in the house he seemed to know when the lady was going to pen up the chicks, and as soon as he saw her on her way out he would get up and follow without even having to be called. Incidentally, during the making of this production we had three dogs with us, and but for Laddie, a Labrador, whom we entrusted to the actor who was to appear with him, Moss and Jeff were never out of our presence. They even slept in our rooms, Moss under my bed and Jeff 'neath Mr Relph's. They were perfectly clean and well mannered and no human could be a better room mate.

*Joseph Relph with "Moss", "Bess" and "Jeff"*

The following incidents will illustrate the loyalty, affection and confidence which exists twixt shepherd and sheepdog. Mr Alec Millar, a Scot, was returning from giving displays at the Dublin Spring Show and the cook on the steamer insisted upon taking charge of the dogs in his quarters. One of these dogs, Vim, must have believed that his master had remained ashore, for it is hardly likely that he would have resented the hospitality of the cook, of all people. However, one of the portholes was open and at the first opportunity Vim jumped through it and in the darkness was lost to drown. Vim had a son, Ben, and it is remarkable that a somewhat similar incident should have happened to him. Ben was exported to Australia and during the process of disembarkation he slipped his collar, dashed across the landing stage and jumped into the sea, as though he was taking the first opportunity of trying to escape back to Scotland. However his life was saved by two sailors who immediately put out in a boat and rescued him.

Mr Tom Roberts of Wales, ran his famous Queen at some International Trials held in Hyde Park, London, and when Queen died of a chill some time later a "Daily Express" representative wrote an obituary in which he said that he would always remember her as he last saw her. His words speak for themselves: -
"Queen ... a speck in the distance ... was crouched in the waving grass, head tilted to one side trying very hard to catch the whistle of the command that the wind drowned. She failed at long last and I could swear there were tears in Queen's eyes."

A Dalesman who was very fond of a good crack was crossing the fell one evening with his dog and a few sheep they had collected to take on to the farmstead. En route they had to pass the residence of a friend and our shepherd couldn't resist calling in. Well, the dog, of course, was left outside in charge of the sheep and master went through the scullery into his host's cheerful kitchen. Inside was comfort and good cheer. The fire was bright and the crack was brighter. Thoughts of night descending on the fells outside were fleeting ones. Time passed, until about midnight they were roused from their reveries by the sound of falling, clattering milk churns and pails. When they investigated they found that the faithful dog had tired of waiting outside and so had manoeuvred the sheep, through the door through which master had passed into the scullery and had settled herself at the entrance. Apparently the dog intended to find the shepherd or at least make more sure of having the sheep safe from straying away in the darkness. But at all events it was not going to leave the sheep.

One point I would like to stress and that is that the secret of success with dogs depends largely upon kind treatment. Indeed it is the same with all animals. Not only do I know this from my own personal experiences with animals but I also know it as a result of contacts I have had, too, with trainers of dogs on the stage and in the circus.

Corporal punishment is not needed for properly trained sheepdogs. To them it is a much greater punishment to be put on a lead and not allowed to take part with the other dogs. But, of course, they do not need punishment because they are not spoiled in the first place.

"There is no good flock without a good shepherd, and no good shepherd without a good dog." The Shepherd's motto.

# 14
## COW-DOG

Some dogs, are good cattle-dogs but not so good when it comes to herding sheep, being, too noisy and not having the virtues of steadiness and patience developed to a very high degree.

In the days before speedy motor transport cattle-dogs were the drover's "right hand" when cattle had to be driven to market. Nowadays the beasts are loaded into motor trucks in the farm yard and unloaded at a bay within the market. But in the old days cattle driven along strange roads had an annoying habit of dashing up by-roads and through gaps in hedges and onto lawns and flower beds of householders who had absentmindedly left open their garden gates. This was an era when the cattle-dog was in his hey-day. He was absolutely indispensable in order to keep the wayward beasts 'on their course' 'til the market pen was gained.

*"Bell" - author's faithful boyhood cow-dog*

A very special cow-dog was "Bell". She was beautiful, being coloured white and a deep rich brown. She had kind eyes and her face reflected her pleasant personality. Bell became the constant and loyal companion of a certain little boy when she was purchased by the lad's father to become foster mother to a valuable litter of Pointer puppies. Everyone who knew her said that they had never known a dog which was a better mother.

People who saw her out walking with the boy would remark, "What a lovely dog," and such remarks used to make the proud little owner's heart put in an extra beat or two.

Wherever that boy went there Bell would go. They were seldom parted. She would guard him and keep him company in the house. If they were in a field together and a stranger appeared in the distance she would know at once and with a few warning barks set herself on guard. Her little master could roll her about, wrestle with her and allow her to roll him about, so well did they understand each other, and there was never the slightest risk that she would so much as "hurt a feather in his wing" even if he accidentally happened to pull an ear a little too hard.

She would turn any cow, however savage or determined it might be, and she could round up any number of cows, taking a big sweep around the herd at terrific speed. But once she got them on the move in the direction required she would let them settle into an unhurried stroll for it does cattle harm to hasten and flurry them. Provided the gates were open, Bell could be sent off for the cows and bring them safely home, from a field half a mile distant, entirely on her own. Whenever she was placed in charge of cattle she could not be persuaded to leave them until she had them safely in byre or field. And if she had a litter of puppies, as she had on one or two occasions, having completed her mission she would immediately hurry away to attend to her family.

On one occasion she was so intent upon her droving that she was run over by a much too swiftly driven four wheeled, horse-drawn dray. Two iron tyred wheels passed over her middle. Suffering from sudden shock and pain she slipped through a hedge, ran away and hid for a night and a day in a wood. It was thought that she might have gone away to die, but, happily, the misery of her young master turned to joy when, unexpectedly, his pet appeared wagging her tail, snuggled her smooth head against him and offered a paw. Ever after this incident she would always get over the hedge into a field whenever she met a vehicle on the road and wait there until it had got safely past, when she would come back once again and resume her duties. But that accident left a small lump on her back and another on her belly. This latter grew in her old age and caused her death.

Now at one time in her career Bell became accused of engaging upon rabbit poaching expeditions. Of course young master would never admit that such accusations could possibly have any foundation in fact. Evidence was only circumstantial. But he would say, a little proudly, that his dog could course a rabbit and just at the moment when she would be about to overtake and snatch it he could stop her and allow the rabbit to go free, so obedient was she to his commands. Suspicions of these escapades arose because on occasions when she went out with someone other than her owner she would sometimes slip away unnoticed and be lost for the day, although she never did such-like when with her young master. In fact if her master was anywhere about she would not accompany anyone else, or if she did happen to be with anyone else and master appeared on the scene she would leave them to join him. Usually when she did take off she would be found sitting in the field with the cows. If she was not there and not back by nightfall young master would stand on the hill and whistle what he called his special 'appealing' whistle, and in a few moments his cow-dog was brushing the calves of his legs.

When he grew into a school youth that young dog-owner was presented with a bicycle which he would ride in front of the cows whilst Bell drove them behind. On occasions, just to show what a clever dog he did possess he would ride away out of sight and let Bell be in sole charge of the cows for the remainder of the journey.

Beneath an elm tree four stones mark the corners of her grave, placed with happy memories of the boyhood companionship of a kind and faithful cow-dog.

Bell belonged to none other than the writer of this story.

# 15
## LAMBING TIME

I don't know if it would be right to call the lambing season a harvest-time but, at any rate, we do speak of the new-born lambs as a "crop". In fact, they represent the first crop of the year, although the real harvest from sheep is, of course, their wool and their mutton.

When lambs are now being born day and night it is a busy time for the shepherds. Shep's first thought in a morning is to get out to the flock as soon as daylight is breaking for he's got to be ready to do a mid-wife's job should any ewes be in difficulty. Then he must keep giving an eye to them as often as possible throughout the day and at night time go round with a lamp to have a look at them.

Those first few drops of rich, thick, sticky milk make all the difference to a newly born lamb. Once it has got upon its feet and had a suckle at the "pantry" then Shep can feel satisfied that it will live and thrive.

And thrive lambs will, provided the ewes can keep up their milk supplies. To help them do this we change them on to a new pasture now and again, because at this time of year they can nibble it off as fast as it grows. We also feed them some dry feeding stuffs twice a day in long wooden troughs.

*Author and daughter Margaret Ann with early Suffolk lambs*

Once the lambs are a few days old they soon learn to help themselves at the troughs, too. In fact lambs are pretty cute at seeking what's good to eat. They find all the tender shoots of grasses that grow close in under the shelter of the hedgerows, for instance. And, if there's any space at all, they push their little heads through to reach what's on the other side – and then they'll crawl through on their knees, and make a gap. Of course, as soon as they do that we block the gap up. But once they've got a taste of something sweet on the other side of the hedge, they're so determined to get to it again that it becomes a real problem to keep them in their own field. And as time goes on they encourage their mothers to follow them!

In order to prevent them from straying like this, a lot of time during the couple of months before they are born is spent in hedging. Next time you're in the country just take a look at a hedge that's been "felled" - that is chopped – and "laid", as we say. Notice that the hedgerow trees have been chopped near the earth – not quite cut through – and laid along the top of the dyke or bank. There are different styles of hedging in different districts but the purpose is the same. The idea is to encourage the hedge to grow thick at the bottom so that nothing can break through – leaving no spaces for the lambs to poke their heads through.

"Close enough to keep a rabbit out", as we say! Now, you'll notice, also, that on each side of the laid branches – known as "Runners" – the bank has been pricked with twigs so that, in effect, a temporary, artificial, or camouflage hedge has been made. In time these branches will wither and rot away but, in the meantime, they're strong enough and prickly to keep the lambs not only from getting into the next field but to prevent them nibbling the new shoots which will soon burst from the buds on runners. And those new shoots, so protected, will in time form the new hedge.

For the first two or three days lambs don't venture far away from their mothers and, after suckling, spend a lot of time sleeping. Pairs of twins lie asleep for hours snuggled together in some wind-sheltered spot or in the warm sunshine. Then, when they're a little older, at each sunset when the air becomes chilly, all the lambs gather together – almost as if by arrangement – and they all go scampering, helter, skelter, to and fro across the top of the field. They have grand fun – from the field gate, across the field, up a little hillock and back again. A brief pause – and off they go again. It's fun watching them.

But it's an anxious time. This frolic can so easily be turned into tragedy. There's such a danger nowadays of a stray dog peeping through that gate and deciding to join in the fun. But for the menace of stray dogs many more farmers would keep sheep. Now, some folk are quite shocked at any suggestion that their dogs might become sheep worriers but, you know, it's always the dog's owner who is to blame. The spoiled dog, pampered by the whole family, is just as dangerous as the family pet which nobody finds time to exercise and which is turned loose to pass time away on his own.

Scampering lambs are a temptation to wayward dogs. When dogs join in the chase they strike terror into lambs and ewes. One snap and a mouthful of wool is not unlike the fun a spoiled dog has at home with father's slipper! And one pull at a fleece leads to another. Then a piece of flesh comes away and warm blood flows. I've caught them at it. And if every dog owner will only think what its like to find a sad little lamb plaintively bleating over the mutilated body of its dead mother and, a few yards away its twin lying with its curly fleece torn from its throat – maybe they'll take more care.

# 16
# THE WOOL CLIP

*"Fleece carriers" Margery and Isobel Ridley*

There's a gathering of flocks for the annual sheep clipping festival. I went out with Harry who'd come along, like all the other neighbours, to give son Tom a hand with his flock of Scotch Blackface sheep.

He bade his dog round them up…. "Git away Don, 'way Don, me lad, Don. Good lad!"

We brought them into Tom's yard and there the ewes and lambs were separated. They remained separated most of the day, until the ewes had been clipped, and the lambs had been dosed as a prevention against worms, and dipped in a special disinfectant solution which would ward off the maggot flies. There was a constant chorus of bleats – ewe calling lamb and lamb calling ewe.

Sheep clipping is an annual event, and for generations has been held on each farm on the same day of the year, weather permitting. There was a team of fourteen to help Tom harvest his wool crop. Eight of them were clipping a sheep each, one was marking them with the "smit" (or paint) marks which are distinctive to Tom's flock, and which are registered in the Shepherd's Flock Book.

One old gentleman kept the pot of "smit" boiling, and, as each ewe was brought to him, after being clipped, he applied his marker.

The shearers sat round a yard on long low stools upon which the catchers kept them supplied with ewes to clip. They have good method, these farmers – no time and motion studies towards efficiency are needed by them. As soon as the wool is off a sheep, there is a man to carry the fleece to the wrappers who do their job as neatly as if they were folding a parcel. Apparently, wrapping fleeces is an old man's job. At least, old William implied as much, for he soon relieved a younger man of that duty by saying "Aa would like to see thee doing summat wi' a bit mair graft in it!"

By each man doing a specific job, the sheep were being clipped at the rate of sixty to seventy an hour. There was good humorous conversation all the time. The monotony of the job was eliminated. In fact, it was fun doing hard work.

It's a big day for the womenfolk, too. Tom's wife had eight ladies from neighbouring farms to help her with the catering. In all there were six meals before all the ewes, looking so different in their undies, were returned to their lambs. And when they did return to their lambs, the poor ewes were greatly perturbed to find that their own offspring didn't recognize them for quite a long time in the new look.

It takes a whole week to clip Tom's flock and on the last day all the hard work is rounded off with a dance in the big barn at night and that's what we call "A reet guid do".

# 17
## DIPPING

Dipping sheep isn't one of the pleasant jobs. It's an uncomfortable wet operation even at the best of times, but when the weather is bad then it can be proper miserable. Miserable enough for men but worse still for the sheep, of course. The law demands that sheep be dipped at least twice a year – once before the end of August and for the second dipping not later than the 15th day of November.

This is because all sheep are liable to harbour a variety of insects and parasites in their fleeces if their wool isn't kept clean. And these insects are always most numerous and active on sheep that, for some reason or other, don't thrive too well. In fact, unless something is done to cleanse them, sheep so affected can become very skinny and even go down.

One of the worst parasitic ailments of sheep is called "scab". Sheep-scab used to be a scourge. Sheep ailing from it would rub against posts and gates in the fields and by contagion the infection was spread from one sheep to another; the parasites multiplying and burrowing under the skin.

It was the seriousness of that disease called "Scab" – as serious in its way as "foot and mouth" – that brought about a law requiring all sheep to be compulsorily dipped twice a year. Every sheep is immersed for at least a minute in a bath of special disinfectant solution which we call "dip". And, usually, the local policeman supervises. Years of following this practice have almost eliminated sheep-scab. Now and again there has been an odd outbreak and whenever that's happened, extra dippings have been carried out under the supervision of veterinary surgeons.

One of the commoner parasites of the sheep's fleece is known as the "ked". Until a few years ago this notorious insect was on almost every sheep and was a standing joke among sheepmen.

It was nothing out of the ordinary to find one crawling up the back of one's neck after being in only passing contact with a sheep! And if you happened to be dressed up in a good suit and sitting in a bus coming away from a sheep sale –

and if there happened to be some misunderstanding townsfolk sitting on the seat behind you – well, you can understand if they took a pretty poor opinion of the cleanliness of farmers!

In recent years, however, thanks be that veterinary scientists – after many years of research – have produced disinfectant dips which have eliminated insects from sheep wool. I've never seen a "ked" or a "louse" on a sheep for years. Modern dips have conquered them. Consequently, the sheep are far more comfortable and happy and thrive better – and we chaps who handle sheep – well, we no longer have to "de-louse" (or "de-ked") ourselves any more. And whilst some sheep, especially if they have soiled fleeces, still do get attacked in warm weather by another pest called the maggot even that enemy isn't the menace it once was.

Well, I started off by telling you what an uncomfortable business this dipping job is. Of course, it's not so bad in the summer – provided there's any summer weather! You see, we gather all the sheep together in a pen and then swim them through a deep concrete bath one at a time. Naturally, some of them splash a bit and the chap who's actually doing the job looks as though he's been in the bath himself when it's all over – usually he's wringing wet! We like a fine day for dipping with a dry breeze – then the sheep don't take any harm. But, by gum, it's a dickens of a job to hit on such a day in November! We don't like dipping in November. You can understand that when a sheep is immersed in the dipping bath for a minute it gets its fleece saturated to the skin. And, you can understand, too, that if the weather's wet, or even just damp, with no drying at all, that sheep's going to remain soaking wet for days. Its body heat will help to evaporate some of the wetness, but it takes a long time to dry out, especially when rain persists for several days after having been dipped.

But for all that, sheep do seem to stand the cold shock of being submerged and the lingering dampness fairly well, and I suppose that brief discomfort is better to bear than feeling itchy for the rest of the year.

Anyway, we're all glad when there's no more dipping until next Summer.

# 18
## WHY SHEEP WANDER

Those little black-and-white lambs which were frolicking on the fells during the summer are quite grown up in the Autumn. We don't call them lambs any longer – we call them "hoggs". They run together in flocks quite separate from their ewes. They're just at that stage of youth when they need good food to make good growth. So it's the flock-masters' practice at this time of year to send them down from the bare mountains to winter on the better lowland pastures where they stay until about the second week in April when, if Nature isn't ungenerous, we can expect enough herbage to satisfy them on the mountains again.

Now these sheep are great wanderers. Yet, there's a limit to their wandering. The peculiar thing is that on their native heath, they confine themselves to a limited range.

As an example, let me tell you about the Herdwick sheep which are a breed peculiar to the Lake District. You'll not find Herdwicks anywhere else in the world. They roam all over the place when they're pastured on the enclosed fields of a lowland farm, yet they never, of their own accord, leave the mountain heath upon which each flock has been bred for generations.

One fine day as I sat alone on a Lakeland mountain top – up among the Herdwicks – and thought about them, it became no wonder to me why they are so contrary.

For the sheep, the mountain, doubtless, provided all that I enjoyed, plus a great deal more. For one thing, the mountain provided a home, and, for another, it provided food. And I thought that if a human being could accept such a home and such food, then, of course, he wouldn't need to come down, but could stay with the Herdwicks! However, we're not made that way, though if food and shelter can be produced, then I think there's something to be said for life as a mountain hermit!

Well, as I sat there thinking and watching, I felt I could really understand the Herdwick's homing instinct. First of all, a mountain is a vast expanse of land,

and it takes quite a long time to get to know it thoroughly if you're going to nose your way over it inch by inch, nibbling the grasses and bleaberry "wire". And, as you thus explore it, as every mountain sheep will, you'll store away memories of the sweetest patches, and of springs and streams, and of crags and boulders where you could shelter cosily from the wind and the rain.

And to all those places sometime you'd have the urge to return. Also, still supposing you were a Herdwick, your mother would have taken you to all these places when you were a lamb; and your grandmother, and your great-grandmother, and your antecedents for generations back would all have done the same thing – drank at the same springs, sheltered behind the same rocks, grazed the same grasses and bleaberry patches, and gazed over the same views.

Well, it's quite true that while there's pasture on the height, the Herdwicks never think of coming down, but the lowlands with all their better grassland are inadequate to keep the Herdwicks from their rugged mountain domain. When spring comes, they'll roam away from even the greenest meadow. They make themselves sheer humbug, and bane of any lowland farmer's life. Neither they nor he can be happy until they're back on the fells again.

Whilst they may not venture on to a strange mountain, they show no reluctance to wander from one lowland field to another nibbling a bit here, and another mouthful there, but never settling to eat their fill, and getting miles away from where they should be.

This "ratching" – that's the shepherd's word for it – this "ratching" is understandable to me now because one of the delights of being on a mountain is the ever-present element of surprise. That in itself is what makes a human being keep on climbing. Over every knoll, and round every crag, there stretches before you a vista, and, if you were a sheep, you'd find a choice bit of herbage which made the exploration worth while. So, I say, little wonder then that a mountaineering Herdwick becomes bored and unsettled with a delectable lowland pasture, where one can fill the stomach with no more effort or adventure than bending down and eating and – having done so – can then only lie there gazing at the boundary hedge!

# 19

## SORTING OUT STRAYS

You might think that the many flocks of sheep roaming the mountains would get all mixed up.... But they don't. Each fell farm has belonging to it a flock of what are called 'heaf-going' sheep. When a farmer takes over a farm he gets the flock with it. And when he leaves, the flock is left the same size as when he originally took over.

Now, the peculiar thing is that each flock stays to its own native heath – generation after generation. Only odd sheep suffer from a lust for wandering beyond their home ground.

Each flock is known by the name of the farm to which it belongs, such as – Wallthwaite, Glencoyne, Birkett Bank, and so on. And each flock has its own distinctive marks applied to each sheep.

Sheep marks are of two kinds. Every hill flock has its own distinctive ear and fleece marks … just in the same way as herds of cattle on American ranches have distinctive brand marks … Bar X, Double Ring and so on. As a matter of fact flock marks sound every bit as romantic. And all these recognition signs are recorded in the Shepherd's Flock Book. When a shepherd finds a stray among his sheep, if he does not recognise it from memory he can look up the Flock Book and find out exactly to which flock that sheep belongs.

The fleece mark of one flock I know is called the "Bugle-horn". It's a tar mark painted from the root of the tail, half way along the back and down the far side. Another example is a "pop" on the tailroot and a stroke across the saddle.

These marks are daubed on with "smit". "Smit" is usually a mixture of tar and brown grease called sheep-salve. It's boiled up in a pot at clipping time and painted on as soon as the sheep have been clipped.

Woollen manufacturers object to shepherds using tar because it's difficult to scour out. But shepherds say that tar is durable and doesn't rub off among bracken.

Ear marks are a double check for recognition purposes and are certainly permanent. The "smit" marks are easily distinguished at a distance but when the sheep are huddled together in a fold you cannot see them. Then it's only by looking at their ears that you can really tell if there are any strangers in the flock. A typical earmark might be described like this; a "slit upper half at far". That means a little incision in the top side of the right ear. If it was "cropped at narr" it would mean the tip of the left ear had been clipped off. Then there is "spoonshank", "keybit", "thumb-bit", "dovetail bit" and many others. They are snipped in (or out!) when sheep are young lambs.

Horned sheep are usually identified by the owner's or the farmstead's initials branded on the horn. These are called "horn burn". A system of notches, or saw marks, on the horns is the shepherd's own reference to the year in which the sheep was lambed.

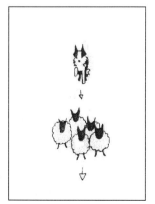

In July and October the shepherds hold what are known as "Meets" – usually on a mountain pass, but in November of every year they select the snugness of some mountain hostelry where they can have the annual "Shepherd's Feast", too. For about a week before the day of the meeting all the shepherds carry out a big round up of their respective flocks and sort out any strays. Then, on the appointed day, each shepherd drives his trespassers to the Meet. All the strays are put into a large pen. The secretary declares, from his knowledge of the markings, which sheep belongs to which flock. "Four there for Goosewell, two frae Lowthwaite, another Goosewell", and so on. As each sheep is declared to belong to a particular flock a shepherd from that flock calls "Aye" – signifying that he's there to claim it. If there happen to be any sheep for return to a flock which hasn't a shepherd representing it, the secretary notes down in his book that the owner is to be fined half-a-crown for each one. A neighbour will volunteer to take the sheep home along with his and deliver them. He'll also collect the half crowns and hand the money to the secretary later.

It's really amazing how shepherds can tell one sheep from another. To some folk all sheep look alike whether or not they have horns, long wool, close wool, are white-faced, "clean" legged, or wearing woolly trousers.

I watched a shepherd crawl on to the top of a two decker wagon. A tarpaulin over the top made it dark inside and the deck was packed with sheep all of one breed. But there was thought to be one in there which ought really to be with another lot. He could remember what it looked like and, crawling on hands and knees among the huddled sheep, he wasn't long until he recognised it in the half light and lifted it out.

Of course, sheep have their own peculiar characteristics and features. Next time you see some just compare their facial expressions and you'll see what I mean. For instance, my brother – who had the eye of an artist – often saw human likeness in the faces of sheep! Perhaps, when referring to some particular sheep, for example, he'd say, "Y'know that ram with the Roman nose that looks like so-and-so _____". And he didn't say it unkindly to suggest that the person was sheepish looking.

Well, to get back to the Shepherds' Meet again. After every shepherd has reclaimed his "lost" sheep, they set off and trek across the fell to be home with their "stragglers" before dusk. But they'll come back again in the evening to round off the Meet with a feast and a sing-song jollification. And the half-crown fines collected from last year's "do" will help to pay for the fun.

Then, in the morning, they'll redaub the smit marks on the returned strays and turn them free again with their own heaf-going flocks on the open mountain.

# 20
## BURNING THE HEATHER

Whenever the weather's dry enough then is the time to burn the heather. Heather-burning on the fells and moors is a form of insurance. Shepherds don't burn it off because they wish to get rid of it. They burn it to improve its quality. It's an insurance against starvation among the sheep flocks in the event of snow lying for any length of time next winter.

The purpose of the burning is to prevent the plants growing very long and woody and tough – growing into, what you might call, miniature "bushes" and "trees". Hill sheep thrive on heather and the practice of burning encourages a new succulent crop to grow in the springtime. And, also, by the time next winter comes and the new tender plants will have made good growth – they'll be sticking up under the snow, if there happens to be any, and when the sheep nuzzle underneath it they'll find something good to nibble and to keep alive on until the weather improves. Every hill farmer likes to have a fair amount of heather on his heath. To him it's a very important crop. Burning it off when it gets rough – and at the right time of year – is really a method of cultivation.

For a long time heather-burning has been a bone of contention between flockmasters and people whose sport is grouse shooting. That's because the shooting men favour plenty of long, strong heather as permanent cover for their birds. However, nowadays the shooters are much more reconciled to the needs of the sheep-farmers. Grouse thrive on heather, too, and, as like as not, they'll thrive better when it's kept sweet and tasty, and there'll still be enough of it to provide cover! Anyway, there are more people who eat mutton than eat grouse!

About the only chap who gets worried about heather fires is the forester, so where heather and timber share a hill-side the burners have to be very careful or else leave that portion to grow wild and rough as delights a shooter.

As I mentioned a moment ago, there's a proper time for burning. It's got to be finished before the end of March. If it went on any later not only the grouse but other wild life would be destroyed, especially at nesting time. This "end of March" date line is now fixed by law. Also, of course, to burn during the spring or summer would be to deprive the flocks of valuable summer forage and the plants would never recover sufficiently and in time to be of any advantage as winter feed.

Well, you can see that native crops like heather – and bleaberry plants, too – certainly reduce the possibility of sheep hungering to death when the countryside is snowbound. Fortunately, snow doesn't usually lie for long periods in this country. Every few years we do have it with us for two or three weeks but it never stays for month after month like some countries have it. So the heather just helps out over that difficult period. If the snow did stay and lie deep for the whole of the wintertime then even the heather wouldn't be much use. All the pasturage would be locked away and – well, just think of any sheep or cattle you may have seen on the lowland farms during a short spell of snow and frost. The poor things just stand there looking all forlorn and feeling cold and hungry until the farmer brings them something to eat from the barn!

If we were to have month after month of hard weather every year we'd have to keep our sheep and all our cattle indoors all winter. That would mean drastically reducing our flocks because there isn't enough space to put all the sheep in the country under cover. Instead of a fell farmer keeping hundreds he would only be able to keep a few dozen. The same thing would apply if there wasn't such a life-saving crop of heather because when deep snow leaves nothing to nuzzle for, animals keep alive on the reserves stored in their own flesh; and that, of course, is starvation diet. So when you see the smoke palls billowing across the moorland skies it means that the hill farmer is as busy with his cultivations as is the arable farmer and his corn drill.

# 21

## STONE WALLS

It would be interesting to know how many thousands of miles of dry stone walls there are in Cumberland and Westmorland. In the county of Kirkcudbrightshire, just across the Solway Firth, there is an estimated 7,000 miles of this durable form of boundary fencing.

Visitors to our Lake District, and particularly those from the wire-and-post fenced flat lands of North America and other places, marvel at our stone wall enclosure system. We take it for granted, but they examine the walls with curious interest and photograph them.

I can understand their curiosity for I have taken the same interest in the timber "snake" fences in Canada built by the Red Indians.

These are made with long lengths of timber split from tree trunks and set up in sections resting on trestled logs where the ends of each section interlock. Just as the stone walls of the fells are held together without mortar or cement so are the Indian timber fences held together without nails or wire or other binding material.

They are called "snake" fences because of their twisting or zig-zag form. The Indians had plenty of timber at hand with which to build their fences whilst, in Cumberland and other mountainous regions our farmers had an abundance of stone.

Wherever stones are to be found throughout the world, dry stone walls were built as the earliest form of land enclosure. The system of walls achieved completeness and there is no extension of them nowadays.

Most were probably erected towards the end of the 17th century and stand today exactly as they were then. Some have fallen into disrepair as a result of damage not being rectified rather than as a result of ravages of time and weather.

A few years ago we viewed with dismay the number of gaps in the walls which were never properly repaired. Some times hasty repairs were made with wire and posts or an even more unsightly mess was made by blocking the hole with a tin sheet or old bedstead.

It seemed that nobody was left who knew how to build stone walls. But the pattern of stone walls erected by our forefathers has established the system of farming on our mountains and moorlands and a gap in a stone wall is equivalent to a breakdown in a piece of farm machinery. It has to be repaired.

Many walling competitions are held in conjunction with local ploughing matches. The importance of the maintenance of dry stone walls is understood and there are today some excellent wallers from as young as 15 years to over seventy years of age.

Dry stone walls have many advantages. First and foremost they are stockproof – which is what a fence is intended to be. They give shelter from the wind and shade from the sun. They require no imported material and can stand on ground where posts cannot be driven into the ground. They cannot be set on fire.

It is interesting to study the construction of a dry wall. Every stone is placed in such a way as to have a duty to its neighbour. All are locked into each other. Wall building is fascinating. One expert I know occupied himself building stone walls in Italy whilst he was a prisoner of war. He built his own house on the Yorkshire moors and trained his school-boy son to be an even better waller than himself.

People wonder how the builders managed to carry all those stones up the fell sides. The answer is that wherever possible on steep slopes the stones were brought down the mountain and not taken up the mountain. They were gathered from screes, perhaps conveniently quarried, gathered loose, and, probably by hammering nearby boulders into pieces.

On more gentle slopes stones would be transported on sledges hauled by fell ponies and dumped ready to be man-handled when required. Stones were regularly gathered from ploughed land and collected into heaps. Many stones are in soil described as "boulder clay". On some soils a "crop" of stones appears with every seasonal ploughing, and every ploughman is glad to have them removed, because a horse ploughman gets a very nasty shock to his body and to the shoulders of his horses every time the plough strikes a "set fast".

The skill of "dry stone dyking" has been passed from father to son among families specialising in the craft.

It is said that some of the walls in Cumbria, Northumberland and Scotland were built by French men who came to this country after the Napoleonic Wars. There is at least one generation of "dry stone dykers" whose family name derives from the French language. Like others of their craft each can look at a dry stone wall and recognise the specific style of the craftsmen who built it.

There are two schools of dry stone walling. The important description of "dry" is, not bound with cement, mortar or other similar based binding substance. The walls are built from the material at hand; no carrying of sand, cement and water up the fell! Of the two schools, the first is to select stones that fit together or "lock-in" from the larger loose stones up to the coping with small stones filling up the middle. Long, broad "throughs" to lay across the middle of the wall are secure binders. A good eye is necessary to match, fit and secure the wall firmly to stand forever.

The second school uses a chipping hammer to shape the stones to make them fit against each other. This man-made to fit method is more applicable on the lower landscapes. One needs not to carry hammers and chisels up the fell side!

In competitions there is a class for hand selected stone work and another for hammer trimmed stone work. For the wall around the garden or farmyard, use of tools and cement is the norm. Such is known is "wet stone walling".

Think of the days spent high up on the mountain; no madding crowd, no traffic, no telephone. But a Border Collie companion, bird song, cool mountain air, a knapsack of bait and a chosen stone for a seat. Look around. The world is at your feet! The walk home is down hill!

# 22
# BIRTH OF A FOAL

*Daisy and Bess*

Daisy was due to foal. The little tell-tale droplets of wax on her teats, for which I had looked every day, had just begun to appear. She might foal any time. So I took her to the little field near the house — we call it the garth – where I could keep an eye on her. There are no gutters or other dangerous places there where a new-born, wobbly foal might tumble and come to harm. No barbed-wire, either ...... darned nasty stuff that "barbarous" wire as we call it. If a foal gets mixed up with that and cuts itself the marks remain with it for life! There was a good bite of lush grass in the garth. I'd saved it specially so that it would be grown sufficiently to last mare and foal at least a month.

I wondered if I should really put Daisy in fresh surroundings for foaling. Some mares are "touchy", y'know. Perhaps, I should have put her in the garth some days before. But then the grass wouldn't have lasted long enough. Anyway, I had confidence in Daisy. She was a grand mare. Sensible... aye, and a bit cunning, too!

Few folk have been lucky enough to see a mare foal. She likes peace and secrecy for the job. You can watch a mare all night, pop into the house for a cup of tea, and as soon as you are safely out of the way she will lie down and drop her foal. Just like that ... a lightening delivery. And, maybe, when you come back the wee begger's on its feet tucking in at the "pantry" good-ho!

Well, I did manage to see Daisy foal. It was daylight and I was a couple of fields distant. She lay down. And just when I thought there was going to be a foal she got up again. That was because a chap with a couple of horses came along the headland on his way to the farm. She waited. Wandered away. Then, when the intruders had gone, she lay down again, and before you could say "Clydesdale" there were two horses where there had been but one! Good job I saw it, too. I could see a pair of spindly legs in white "socks" striking the air. The foal was trying to get out of the "container". It's proper name is sark – an envelope of tough membrane – in which the foal is born. Old Daisy would have got the foal out I suppose, but I was over those two fields like grease lightening, and ...zip! I had that sark from over its head – and its nostrils drew in air. I didn't want it to smother. Daisy just lay there and rested for a while. The foal stretched out its forelegs and pressed its jelly-like hooves to the ground. A shudder seemed to ripple through its body. As though the engine was starting up! It surveyed the "wondrous scene." Daisy indulged in licking and nuzzling for quite a long time. She licked it all over. And in between spasms of licking and nuzzling she paused to nicker. It sounded to me like a happy little chuckle of achievement, satisfaction, approval, contentment. This was Motherhood in its finest hour.

Here was a new life. These soft wide nostrils were drawing in cool morning air. These were the first breaths of possibly millions which that firm, warm little body would respire. I couldn't help but think on these things as I watched this miracle of life. And in the midst of my contemplations - pleasant contemplations they were – I began to laugh. The foal suddenly found its voice. It pricked its ears and nickered. Then the fun started. It sprawled its legs and tried very hard to stand up. I said, "Aye, that's right, get up and have a look round". But I knew there would be something more inviting to stand up for than a better look at the view. Instinct was busy now.

The filly got herself into the most grotesque positions. She put her legs in all the wrong places and flopped down several times. But life is meant to be lived and you can't live it if you don't make good use of your faculties. Eventually, she got her feet in just the right places. She pressed them to the ground, raised her fore-end, got her haunches half way up, wobbled – nearly fell. Gradually she straightened her big knees. And she stood there, swaying unsteadily on her long pasterns, her fetlocks almost touching the ground. She seemed to be wondering which foot to step with first, lest she completely over-balanced. And when she did move a leg and didn't fall – well, it all seemed so easy! She began to walk until she swayed rather frighteningly... but saved her balance just in time and then waited while more strength surged into her tender muscles. Eventually, she "cake-walked" to Daisy, nuzzling her nose all round her mother's body until at last! she found Nature's "pantry", and the sweetest of milk was flushing from the warm black teat as she noisily suckled. All would be well from now on.

I brought a bucket of bran mash for Daisy and the family came out to see the "new-comer". Now what should we call it? The choice of a name is Mother's job. Just then a young lady on her way to work took her usual peep over the hedge. She was expecting to see the new tenant in the garth one of these mornings. And now, at last, here it was…. "Oh, lovely" … So, Mother said "we'll call the foal Bess." And the sparkle of pleasure in that young lady's eyes left no doubt that the birth of a foal really is a happy event.

Now little Bess thrived from the moment she drew that first flush of milk. After her first belly-full, life seemed to be a matter of less urgency.

*Bess*

The milk left a white froth around the sensitive whiskers of her soft lips and nostrils. She looked so funny standing there…. a proper spindle-shanks …. seemingly realising that there were other activities to perform apart from suckling milk. Indeed, there were many challenges to be met. Life would be a big adventure. But, as one old countrywomen said, "Just like anyone of us, with food in her belly, she will have courage to face the devil!"

For the first week or so Bess's life was mainly occupied with sleeping and feeding. Hour after hour she lay stretched out in the warm sunshine… fast asleep. Daisy grazed round about her.

To sit at the window overlooking the garth and watch the pair of them was peacefully thrilling… if you know what I mean? Daisy wore such a benign and contented expression whilst she pulled the lush grass and all the time kept an eye on her thriving offspring. Together they portrayed the essence of "belonging" to each other. And when the old girl had eaten her fill she stood beside the outstretched Bess so that her head hung directly over her little daughter. In that position she dozed, yet ever alert for the moment the foal might awake or that danger might threaten.

Y'know, a foal is a delightful creature. No one who has a soul can help but be fascinated by its antics.

One evening the sky darkened and it began to rain. Now the baby Clydesdale had so far felt nothing touch its body save the caress of warm sunshine and the kiss of its mother's gentle nuzzling. So when the first few drops pelted down on its back she pricked her ears, cocked her head in alarm and did a sprightly prance to escape from this totally unexpected bombardment.

But the rain fell wherever she went... and she didn't like it! She was on her metal! However, even Canute couldn't keep the tide back and, as the rain came on and on she turned, bewildered, to mother and stood right under Daisy's belly. But Daisy, wise as you make 'em had a better idea. She walked quickly down the garth to where the trees overhang in a corner. Bess tripped along beside her and then, with their backs to the storm mother and daughter stood side by side until the shower was ended.

Another funny incident was when she first found out how to roll. She laid down to enjoy one of her usual good stretches. With head and neck extended she found herself almost half-over on to her back. With a little lurch she could wave her legs in the air. This must have been a pleasant sensation. She did it again – and again... and then a bit more vigorously... and this time she couldn't help herself for she flopped right over on to her other side – almost into a sitting position. She didn't expect that! For a few seconds she just sat there shaking her head – as much as to say "Oh dear, where am I?" Then she got up. But she had learnt a new trick and, thereafter, often did a roll over.

As Bess grew up she became inquisitive. I watched her make a lone expedition to a corner of the field. She began to investigate whatever, in her curiosity, she considered an object of interest. Of a sudden, as though realising she was all by herself, she scampered back to Ma, rubbed against her and slid between her legs. And as Ma walked away she passed in front of her, under her neck, pressed against her shoulders and stopped her in order to partake of a quick one – just to fortify herself for the next adventure!

Sometimes Daisy herself would loll in the sunshine and enjoy an afternoon siesta. And when Bess felt hungry she nuzzled the mare as she lay there and impatiently pawed her, beckoning that she get up because it was baby's milk time!

Nature didn't intend her to eat much solid food too soon. She hadn't a long enough neck to reach the grass... her legs were too long for her to reach low enough. All she could do was to attempt little sharp snatches at tufts by bending a knee or standing astride.

I thought it was a good idea to make friends with Bess early. So I went into the garth and stood quietly not far away from the mare. After a while Bess came towards me. Each day she seemed to get bolder. When she was near enough I held out my hand. She came up bravely… Even followed me when I walked away. But when we got farther away from Ma than usual she lost confidence, whipped round and scooted off back again. Once she nuzzled my hand but cringed away with a shudder as soon as I touched her with my other. But when my hand was smeared with honey then she developed cupboard love and I fondled her and rubbed her behind her ears… she liked that!

Once, as she lay asleep, I crawled up to her on my hands and knees and stroked my flat hand over her body before she realised it was me. Up she got in such a hasty way as to imply that my behaviour was outrageous! Ultimately, I did gain her confidence and she would allow me to lift each of her feet off the ground in turn.

We indulged in this hob-nobbing every day. And then our relations became somewhat strained. It was time to further the young lady's education. She was about three months old by now. I slipped a halter over her head. She resented it forcibly. She ran away from me but I had a long rope fastened to the halter and I clung to it. Sticking my heels into the ground. She pulled and jerked with all the power in her compact little body. And when she found that pulling didn't release her she made rushes at me – punching the air with her fore-legs. Still I hung on. She submitted… and I petted her again. Before long she acquiesced and even enjoyed being led around.

But Bess was always thinking about her mother. She nickered violently when Daisy was left in the stable and Daisy replied in no less agitation. Indeed, the foal was very chary about being led away unaccompanied by her dam. Every few minutes she became fractious. It was a job to lead her past a herd of cows once. She wanted to follow them and she looked quite perky and surprised when, with the light of admiration in his eyes, the drover walked over to her and said in his old countryman's way: "Ah, da little baba!"

Feeding, sleeping, sniffing odd corners of the garth and exercising. That was the foal's day. Invariably in the cool of the evening and again in the freshness of the morning, in accordance with the ways of Nature, she took her twice-daily exercise. Round and round the field she scampered – flat out – full speed. Then trot back to mother and brush against her flanks.

After that, each eventide, they both took shelter in the lee of a hedge. And every new day they greeted with the joy of life. It did my heart good to watch them.

# 23

## A VIEW FROM THE SADDLE

Throw your leg over a pony and, in the words of one North Country poet, you have –

> *"A wide world for a Kingdom,*
> *And a saddle for a throne."*

Mounted on horseback is just about the ideal way of seeing the countryside. Not only can you see over the hedgerows – and leisurely notice everything – but, if you're on the right type of pony, the wild and rugged wide-open-spaces are yours to travel in comfort and safety; the less frequented places, where a car can't get, or even a bike with any comfort; where there aren't any roads, or even tracks, at all.

The right type of pony, of course, is one of the native breeds. And, in the North Country, my choice is the Fell pony. They're grand to ride and are the safest means of transport over mountain, moor and marsh. They have a wonderful realisation of the moment danger exists. So safe, even in a fog, that you couldn't force one in any direction along which it sensed that danger lurked. They're as tough as their rugged domain and nippy enough to avoid any awkward spots – such as a bog or a precipice.

Lots of places it wouldn't be fair to attempt on horseback; but the people who laid the roads, and passes, and bridle paths were sensible enough to fashion them along the valleys and avoid going over the steep tops. The air is fresh on the mountains and it's lonesome. You can't help but appreciate the companionship of your pony. And the man-made frailties of the daily world seem remote and foreign. Y'know it's a wonderful sensation to ride along the heights – particularly in Lakeland. The charm and inspiration of the country is below and around you – yours to gaze upon. Halt in your journey of a calm and peaceful evening and all that breaks your own silence is a gentle creaking of the pigskin saddle. Away to the west'ard, across the Solway Firth, is a multi-coloured sky painted by a setting sun. There's the distant, ringing laughter of children at play down in the valley and across the ling comes the occasional bleat of a ewe and its lamb, and a grouse calls "Come back, come back, come back." When the air

*Pony trekking in Ennerdale*

becomes chilled it's good to feel the warmth of the body between your legs. Whilst you ride back home the countryside settles down for the night. A blackbird pipes the world to sleep. If you listen carefully you may hear the purring of the "croaker's chorus" in the background; - down by the pond the frogs are at "Choir practice!"

Back at the stable you give your pony a brisk rub down with a wisp of straw. Then, having watered, fed him, and made him cosy for the night you go and fill your own "inner man".

As you settle to sleep with happy thoughts of the day's ride, so, too, does your mount. And next morning, bright and early, the skylark will fill the air with joyful accompaniment as, once again, you ride out in the open.

# 24

# FELL GALLOWAY ROUNDUP

*Lingcropper*

There is a round-up time on the fells in December. Not of the flocks of sheep but – and perhaps you'd never guess! – the Fell Ponies are rounded up.

In Cumberland we call these horses the "laal fell galloways". We don't really know how they first became established on the fells, but there's a story about how one strain was introduced which probably has some truth in it.

It was after one of the numerous skirmishes during the Border Wars that a handsome stallion, saddled and bridled, was found straying on Stainmore. His warrior master had likely met with the extreme penalty. Well, it was a farmer who found this stallion and he took him home. He gave him the name of "Lingcropper" – because he found him "cropping the ling", or, in other words, "grazing the heather"!

Nowadays he's spoken of quite reverently as Old Lingcropper because from him is descended one of the most famous lines of pedigree fell ponies. And his name is still handed down from generation to generation of his line. There are, or have been, several "Lingcroppers" – Brown Lingcropper, Black Lingcropper, and so on.

At a guess, Old Lingcropper was probably ridden across the Border from Galloway – so we can see how the name Fell Galloway was derived.

Fell Ponies are one of the hardiest and most useful breeds of "all-rounder" horses to be found. Sure-footed, compact and powerful, a fell pony has never been known to bear a natural blemish or unsoundness. They do jobs over rough mountain country which larger breeds and even tractors couldn't tackle. And they're grand riding ponies. Certainly the quickest means of transport over rocky mountain and moor and marsh.

This "nippiness", as we call it, makes them capable of being schooled into good gymkhana ponies. They're extremely friendly little beasts and there's a big demand for them (at present) as riding ponies for children and elderly people – yes, and for folk who are a bit over-weight too. You, see, a fell pony will carry a sixteen stone man quite easily and as they're only from fifty-two to fifty-six inches high you haven't far to step up to mount, or, on the other hand, far to come down if you fall off!

Now, this rounding-up business isn't the Wild West Rodeo you might expect. It's all done very quietly and leisurely. Perhaps a couple of fellows will ride round on horseback but the other shepherds will go out on foot and, spreading themselves out, just advance and manoeuvre the herd gently down to the farmyard.

Actually, the December round-up is the second. The earlier one was at the end of October when the foals were weaned from the mares. Of course, there was a bit more excitement then. It wasn't any use merely herding them into the farmyard. They had to be got into a building with a roof, because once you've got the mares sorted out and the foals left behind, the lish little things will either jump or climb out of anywhere that hasn't got a top on it to keep them in! So anxious are they to get back to their mothers.

This present round-up which always takes place before Christmas is for the sake of moving the herd down to better pastures before there's any heavy snow fall which might lie a long time. And whilst the job is on, several ponies will be picked out for breaking-in and schooling during the winter months.

Fell ponies live till well over thirty years of age, and many tales are told of their achievements. Before the railway was laid, a fell pony stallion used to run the mail from Penrith to Keswick and back – a distance of eighteen miles each way – daily for eleven years. A rider on another one left Exeter at the same time as the stage coach to London, and riding the one pony, beat the coach to London, although the coach horses were changed no fewer than fifteen times during the journey. A distance of a hundred-and-sixty-eight miles. So that all goes to show of what grand stuff these "laal fell galloways" are made.

# 25
# HORSE CHARMERS

*"Horse Charmers"*

Horses are like elephants, they never forget. It's doubtful if any horse has ever been permanently cured of a vice. It may be subdued for a time but it will never do to trust. Restiveness in horses may be the effect of bad temper, which may be a natural disposition. More likely it's the result of improper breaking or training. Such wicked traits as rearing, kicking, plunging, biting, bolting, running back or standing stock still are mostly the fault of the human element. They are caused by neglect, impatience, or misunderstanding during early life when the horse's character is being moulded, and when it should be learning to have confidence in its master. If it is first given confidence it won't fear any experiences it has to endure during its training, or, for that matter, during its life.

Horses buck and plunge and all the rest, as a means of defence because they are frightened. A horse's first line of defence is its speed – to get away from trouble as fast as possible. It adopts all kinds of contortionist tricks, and kicks with both hind and front feet, when the situation gets desperate.

When you find seasoned horses which, for example, won't stand tied up or won't pass through a stable doorway then you can bet that such vices are the results of frightening experiences, the memories of which have become firmly planted. To diagnose the cause of such troubles is an exercise in psychology. For instance, perhaps, at one time when that horse was entering a doorway the door might have swung to and bashed it on the head. Now the problem is how to regain that horse's confidence so that it won't jib at passing through a doorway.

There have been quite a number of people in the past who were supposed to possess a secret mystic power of being able to cure or tame difficult horses.

In the early nineteenth century there lived in Yorkshire a famous colt-breaker nick-named "Jumper". This chap even tamed a buffalo and a pair of reindeer for the saddle. One horse, sent to him, wouldn't have anything placed upon its back. It would lie down and try to roll. In ten days "Jumper" had the horse so tame that it would carry anything and even lie down and get up when he commanded. For about seven months its manners stayed perfect. Then it was turned out to grass for a summer and afterwards it again became unmanageable.

"Jumper's" system seems to have been one of brute force and fearlessness. He began by being rough and it's said that his encounters with restive animals caused him to have nearly every bone in his body broken during his time. He must have been something of a hypnotist too. On one occasion his unusual methods failed on an unruly horse. So he stood on the near side and forcibly pulled the off-rain until the horse's head was drawn back to the off-shoulder. And he sternly stared over the withers into the animals eyes for several minutes. Soon the horse began to tremble and perspire. Then "Jumper" let go and after a few pats and a little coaxing his patient followed him around like a pet.

The most famous of all horse-charmers was an Irishman called the "Whisperer" whose real name was Sullivan. His methods are cloaked in an air of mystery.

There was a horse called "King Pippin" entered to run at the April meeting of 1804 on the Curragh. He was extraordinarily vicious and his particular vice was biting and worrying anyone within reach. He would even tear at the leg of his rider. On this occasion he was absolutely unmanageable. They couldn't even get the bridle on him. So, the services of the "Whisperer" were called. He had himself shut in a box with the horse for the whole of the night. Next morning out he stepped with "King Pippin" following him like a lamb. He would lie down on "Whisperer's" command and also allow his mouth to be opened and any person's hand to be put inside. He won a race at that meeting.

But even "Whisperer" couldn't permanently cure a wicked horse. "King Pippin" remained docile for about three years, broke away again, killed a man and had to be shot.

The "Whisperer" never divulged the secret of his art nor even mentioned how he came by it. He could usually charm a restive animal in about half an hour. It was said that the secret of his charm was a whisper. All that anyone knew about his method was that he and the horse were shut in a stable until he gave the signal for the door to be opened. Then he would be found lying side by side with the horse playing as though it were but a kitten. And there was never noise or bustle whilst they were inside.

Sullivan's secret must have died with him for he had a son who, although he was sought as a horse-breaker at times, was never so successful as his father. Sometimes the horses took no notice of him at all.

"Whisperer" and "Jumper" specialised in methods of breaking horses of bad habits already acquired – they didn't seem to be very scientific – and now, let's contrast their ways with those of a couple of other people who specialised in training horses from foalhood so that they grew up without faults.

There was a Madame Isabelle, famous throughout the Continent, who once broke in a horse at the Cavalry Depot at Maidstone in six lessons. She believed in gentleness as opposed to severity. She declared – what I believe to be a great truth – that horses are rendered vicious "from injustice and brutality of which they have been victims". She invented two pieces of equipment which served as a "dumb jockey". Using these she claimed to have a horse thoroughly trained in twenty-seven lessons and fit for being ridden out in only twelve lessons.

An American trainer, a Mr Rarey, relied almost completely upon gaining a horse's confidence by gentleness and kindness. It is a similar system to that used by many people today. And I've proved its effectiveness myself.

He set out to gain the trust of the horse by having it in his sole presence as often as possible. He spoke softly, allowed the youngster to smell his hands. Then he handled it all over, starting with the head, neck and so on, until, eventually, he could raise each foot off the ground without any trouble. If the horse did become restive he would strap up its fore-legs and bring it down with the handling. He would sit on various parts of the horse whilst it laid there. Gradually, he would introduce items of harness – a little at a time – until it had no fear of anything he did or put upon its back.

# 26
# "BOXING" HORSES

Like all other animals, horses possess an instinctive ability to defend themselves. Out in the open their first line of defence is speed to get far away from the trouble. But in other situations, such as in stable or harness, defence can be aggressive biting or kicking with hind feet. If the defence is against the aggression of another horse then biting is augmented by standing high on hind legs and punching with forefeet in a "boxing" fight. Amongst smaller animals, hares are notable experts of stand-up boxing fights.

Early in the last century there was a serious fight between two stallions at Stud Farm, near Camerton, in West Cumberland. Stud Farm was in the occupation of the Steele family whose main business was keeping horses at stud. They had seventeen or eighteen entire horses most of which travelled the county serving mares at the farms. The stud was well known for its Clydesdales and included two or three Hackneys and two or three race horses.

The horses that did battle were a brown racehorse stallion called "Ale" and a brown hackney stallion called "Sensation". They were being exercised by two young boys and it was on the brow above Flimby and just below the old Gillhead Colliery that they happened to get a bit too near to each other. They reared, broke loose from the boys and had a real fight. They viciously bit each other and, standing on their hind legs punched at each other like a pair of boxers.

Eventually some of the grooms arrived on the scene from the farm and succeeded in parting the combatants without getting hurt themselves.

The stallions were not much worse for the experience and both travelled at stud afterwards.

# 27

## SEQUENCE

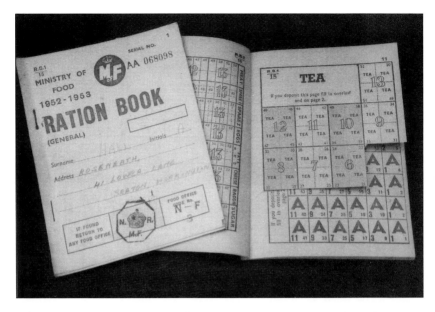

I n country life, with all that is around us, we share nature's environment; birds and animals of field and woodland, hedgerows, streams, lakes, dales, mountains, plants and flowers. They all claim our permanent and curious attention. Constituents of the environment are the essence of a common interest that generates fellowship among country folk engrossed in the fundamental husbandry of land to grow food. Whether we live far apart or nearby we labour in peaceful occupation with nature to preserve life from hunger.

I recall the peaceful labour of a long and late finishing haytime in the year 1939. The final rakings were gleaned at the end of August; within three September days World War II was declared, and life became no longer peaceful. Next to be harvested were corn and root crops; the first of seven under wartime regulations. But the next six came from more acres than farmers had ever ploughed before. From that melancholy September day a manifold change overtook British agriculture.

The sea lanes along which ships brought wheat and other products were beset by enemy submarines. Eventually, there was a daily toll of ships sunk. Every citizen was issued with a book of ration coupons for food and clothing. Petrol coupons were available for essential motoring only. The Government order was "Dig for Victory". Farmers had to plough every acre that might grow a crop; even moorland and golf courses, and home gardens grew more vegetables.

Fortunately, some ships, in convoy, bringing tractors and ploughs from America, and some fuel oils, slipped through the blockade. Thus did the new-fangled tractor machine come to join forces with our long-serving trusty farm horses in the extensive "Ploughing Up Campaign". Never before did a nation more desperately realise that mankind's most precious asset is soil! Long rested meadows and other permanent grassland which had not been ploughed for many years proved exceptionally fertile and produced abundant crops.

The traditional five-year organic crop rotation system was not strictly abided by, which was:

    From grass
    to cereals (1)
    to roots (2)
    to cereals undersown with a mixture of selected grass seeds (3)
    to hay (4)
    to grazing again in 5th year (5).

It was not a good plan to break the sequence, but in wartime risks are taken. In expedient and unusual ways farming maintained food for the nation.

As a result of the war, tractor power quickly replaced live horse power. A generation of horse-lovers who may have admired the round-the-clock work ability of the tractor in the emergency, were not necessarily impressed with the quality of the initial and elementary work of the new-fangled mechanism! With not a little heartache did they see the out-pacing of their flesh and bone workforce of sensitive and gentle giants, possessed of fond attachment and mutual understanding.

Connoisseurs of those early "vintage" tractors who keep them in showground trim also retain a sentiment for their treasures. But their sentiment cannot really be so deep as the affection of a "vintage" horseman for his equine quadruped to whom he could talk and be understood.

Although the war ended in 1945, and peace was declared, it was not until June 1946 that a so-called day of "Victory" was celebrated. Rationing continued until the end of 1953.

# 28
## APPRECIATION DAY

The countryside looked lovely in the sunny morning freshness of the day chosen to be called "Victory Day". The corn and grass crops showed their appreciation of the few odd showers, recently enjoyed during six months of remarkable dry weather, by blooming a healthier green. One felt that nature would yet restore the yellowy, wilting leaf of the cereal to show better prospects of a promising harvest. The clovers and trefoil were starting to crowd at the feet of the taller rye grass and cocksfoot, thickening the hay crop in the bottom, to ensure the next rains would not easily be droughted from the ground by dry winds and baking sunshine. Nature was in happy mood and the plants were appreciative.

A fuller bite on the grazings meant that livestock could lie down with full bellies even earlier in the morning, contentedly chew their cuds (if cattle or sheep) and appreciatively contemplate their pastures. A happy change from the constant nibbling of bared fields; a change from the mere appeasement of hunger to one indicative of thriving. There was a great peacefulness this morning, and nature had adorned her charm with colour. The quiet Solway reflected a blue sky and gondolas of white cumulus clouds seemed motionless as monuments above the Scottish hills. Then away to the north, and before the mouth of the Nith there came a speck of white on the blue backcloth of sea. Soon it stood, tall and monumental, appearing to grow as it sped nearer. It didn't take long to recognise the graceful lines of a tall-masted racing yacht. All her milk-white canvas was aloft, gathering the sea-breeze, and her hull was milk-white too. Probably she was sailing to Liverpool to take part in the midnight race to the Isle of Man. So the beauty of the morning was even further crowned and I felt that those yachtsmen must surely be appreciating the freedom of the sea and the peace there was.

This I felt, was "Appreciation Day". It seemed silly to call it "Victory Day" when I remembered that the peoples of the world suffer from hunger and want, suspicion and jealousy. This morning seemed to remind us of what a pleasant world we do live in if only we really appreciated that fact. It felt so naturally comfortable to be alive in such conditions. The trials and tribulations of mankind were assuredly foreign to the Christian way of life available to us.

It was good to contemplate quietly many things deserving of our appreciation. The yachtsmen could play a fair game of skill with nature's breezes without fear of man-strewn death traps along their course. We could appreciate that no longer was there a mass slaughtering of our fellows. Also, we could lament the wickedness of man which led to the oversoon passing of our dear ones from a world that could be so comfortable for us all as this pleasant morning suggested. There was much to appreciate in the knowledge that however mankind ravaged itself and its properties the good earth still remained the source of life and hope of the future. And so it would do for all time; even if man split the wrong atom – the lighter atom before he knew how to control it, and eliminated himself and his work.

The soil will never, of its own accord, let us down. The danger is that we shall let it down by an abuse of its fertility. By a makeshift policy of crop rotation, yielding from hand to mouth in annually decreasing returns. Such is the food production policy the world is having to adopt. It is a dangerous one that does not cater for livestock and muck. Without them corn will yellow and wilt, even in a good season. Famine, it would appear has threatened us as retribution for having engaged in world massacre ... because we didn't appreciate the gift of peace and plenty. Now, unless we appreciate the ability of the land and those who work by it, we shall be condoning famine. Retribution for doing so may be a mass dying of our kin until we are reduced in number in proportion to our declining food supplies. The day that crisis is averted will be a Victory Day.

# 29
# .....AND LATER (ABOUT 1954 ONWARDS).....

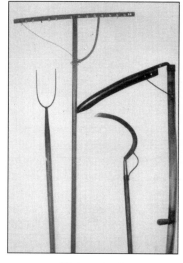

*Vintage tools*

Since the start of the Second World War there have probably been more changes in the practice of agriculture than occurred during the whole of any previous century. The same is probably true in respect of industry and of life and leisure generally. And it all happened in less than the average space of a lifetime.

In times past our ways of doing work were as modern for those times as are our ways of doing work in the present time. The quickness of modernisation within a succession of two generations resulted in a father's work tools becoming classified as "vintage" by his sons and "antiques" by his grandsons.

In making changes we sometimes disregard the method-wisdom passed on by our forefathers from several generations of basic experiences. Consequently, whilst the intention of change is to improve, make easier, speed-up, economise and make money, such changes are not inevitably better in all respects.

The preceding chapters refer to a period when there were three, four and probably more workers on most farms. Such has been the change that farms which once employed a number of staff are now worked by a farmer and his wife with occasional help and seasonal service by a machinery contractor.

Hence, very few farms keep hay forks and rakes, paraffin lamps in the byre or manually operated equipment. All of these are "vintage" if not quite "antique". Where, once upon a time, haycocks and pikes graced a picturesque summer scene there are instead fields dotted with shiny, black plastic bales – like huge balls massed on a massive bowling green – each containing half a tonne of grass cut and parcelled, transported and placed in rows and heaps by machinery. Not

*Corn crop in stooks*

aesthetically attractive in a rural view! Neither, of course, during unfortunate weather was the sight of rain-sodden haycocks! However, there is a problem. What to do with the unusable plastic wrapping when it is removed?

Also disappeared from the harvest scene are rows of stooks in the corn fields, each lined up in a north-south configuration so that sheaves on each side of the stook had equal drying benefit from the morning to afternoon east-south-west directions of the sunshine.

The skill of stooking sheaves became redundant when the combine-harvesters began mowing and threshing in a single operation. Before that, sheaves were carted off and built into neat stacks in which the grain hardened and the straw matured. When the crop was threshed from the stack the accompanying weed seeds were spewed from the threshing drum into a contained heap and eventually burned.

Using a combine harvester the straw is deposited in rows on the stubble to be mechanically picked up and baled but the accompanying weed seeds remain on the field. Consequently, grain crops have to be sprayed with chemical preparations whilst still growing to kill weeds as they emerge. That's why we see those so-called "tramlines" across cereal fields – pathways along which tractors are driven with spraying equipment. Of course, the chemical sprays also destroy aphids and airborne cereal diseases; and, doubtless, some of Nature's other tiny creatures which probably helped to keep crops healthy during the "vintage" farming years.

Haymaking is virtually a "vintage" occupation. Almost all grass grown to be stored for winter fodder is made into silage in those shiny black bags or in pits or clamps. The smell of good silage is not unpleasant. Badly made or poorly constituted silage smells distinctly unpleasant. One problem is to control the silage effluent from seeping into waterways.

After the cows have eaten and digested the silage comes the handling and disposal of that obnoxious bi-product called "slurry". It is all moved mechanically through pipes and pumps into large storage tanks, and from storage tanks into dispersal tankers to be pressure-sprayed on the fields. It is a stinky business. The rural air is horribly polluted.

During the winter when slurry tanks can fill quickly to the risky point of overflow it becomes the job of heavy tractors towing heavy dispersal spreaders to make emergency forays across rain-soaked fields churning the land into deep mud and ruts, compacting and damaging the structure of the sub-soil. This happens at a time when vehicles should be kept off the land, unfortunately.

When slurry is spread during wet weather it is subject to being washed off into drains, ditches and streams. When spread during very dry weather it forms a crust on the surface. The contrast between slurry and solid farm-midden-manure is that the latter was carted on to the fields when land was dry or frozen; it was forked from the cart into rows of equally sized heaps spaced seven yards in each direction, from where it was spread using a hand-held gripe. By this "vintage" method the muck gradually disintegrated into the soil, assisted by indigenous worms and rain showers. It was not sluiced away, nor did it harden into a crust, and soon nascent grass emerged freshly green through the evenly spread crumble. And there was no offensive smell.

During "vintage" equipment years skylarks and corncrakes had time to hatch their chicks before the grass was mown for hay. At dawn and in the evening one heard the corncrake announcing its name and during the day skylarks soared high above and filled the air with their song.

The large leaves of docks, or dockens, which are so useful to rub on the skin to relieve the irritation of nettle sting were used by farmwives as semi-wrapping in which to display decorated one-pound-weight slabs of butter. Unfortunately, docks are deep-rooted, multi-seeded weeds which can propagate and rapidly multiply not only from seeds but also from chips of root and stalk. It was offensive to a farmer's eye to see them in his hayfield and he would pull them out by the roots, dry them in heaps and burn them.

In recent years docks have become a weed crop in profusion. When early grass is cut for silage the dock stalks are already strong enough to root when chopped into pieces and, of course, are included in the silage. During late grass cutting when docks carry seeds they are also included in the silage. Result? They eventually return to the land in slurry and a new growth of docks can be overwhelming in next year's grass crop. Yet again the farm economy has to cope with the expense of applying selective weed-killers.

The "vintage" machinery of the time span covered in preceding chapters included an in-barn winnowing machine, turned by hand, for separating grain from chaff and small seeds. The winnowed grain then went through a crushing, or rolling, mill driven by an oil fired, water cooled engine. The crushed grain, usually oats and barley, was mixed in defined proportions eg. with linseed meal and decorticated cotton seed for cattle feed supplemented with sliced turnips and kale. These rations made up on the farm preceded the expansion of the big milling firms who introduced conveniently bagged, or bulk delivery, concentrated cattle feeds with measured minerals and vitamins, etc. Unfortunately, unbeknown to farmers some feeds were supplemented with high protein produced from some kinds of recycled waste including animal offal. Processed animal offal did not prove to be an agreeable diet for ruminant cows! A process now thankfully prohibited.

The introduction of big field machinery required wider gateways and enlarged fields for working convenience. Hedgerows were uprooted and two or three fields combined into one. This practice upset many farm maps, confusing field ordnance survey numbers and field names. Such farm improvement schemes were subsidised by the Government.

Looking back to long ago when the land enclosure system was established the fields were not so large as they are on most present day farms. At first they would closely surround villages, extend along valley bottoms and waterways, and would be the confined grazing areas of sheep, cattle and horses. There originated a maxim which declared "sheep should not hear the Church bells on two successive Sundays whilst still in the same fields". This required that sheep be frequently moved to fresh pastures.

Since the pulling out of hedgerows to enlarge fields some became inconveniently large for livestock. Therefore, a method of paddock grazing was introduced by dividing large fields into smaller fields with wire fences, thus to return the land to the original purpose of small fields. Once again, having heard the Church bells whilst grazing one paddock they could be grazing another paddock when the bells tolled again the following Sunday! However, wire fences do not provide the shelter of a good hedgerow, nor do they host birds and bees and other small claimants to share Nature's habitat. So, to rectify this situation the Government made another change and provided a subsidy for reinstating field hedgerows.

During the author's boyhood family transport was by horse and trap. Roads had never been built for motor cars. Alas, there is no safe road space left for horse drawn traffic. Neither, we are told, is there space enough for many more motor cars!

Having already discarded horses and horse vehicles what will people do when fuel oils are expended and immobile motor vehicles are abandoned to rust? Before the onset of such a debacle perhaps agriculture will grow crops for fuel oil as well as for food?

*Butter Churn*

*All-weather Digby*

# 30
# ORIGINATION

*Horse Power*

The most basic, precious assets on this earthly globe are air, soil and water. Without these elements there would be no life as we know it. Our planet would be as defunct as a withered apple.

Since the "Beginning", mankind using strong hands and arms, assisted by both bovine and equine power, has laboured to till soil, plant, cultivate and harvest crops to provide food for survival of both man and beast.

Over the ages a stupendous progression of method changes have evolved in the craftsmanship, skill and art of the farmer. From scratching soil with a dibble-stick to making a spade, or a badza to hack with. Then to invent the everlasting plough slicing and turning the earth in orderly fashion that soil shall benefit from climatic influences – sun, rain, frost, wind – in temperate, sub-tropical and tropical lands.

This fundamental tool of agriculture is the universal icon of peaceful endeavour.

Human invention has produced a succession of tools ancillary to the plough to crumble the aerated soil the plough brings to the surface into friable tilth – the preparation of a seed-bed. Examples of original harrows included tough thorn bushes lashed to planks or angled tree branch to be hauled across the ploughed land by either ox or horse. Such crude implements were succeeded by harrows of wooden spikes, iron spikes, and deeper digging tines. Until the sophisticated, automotive powered oscillating/rotating harrows of modern times. All to shred and pulverise the sliced earth into a friable "bed" where sown seeds, planted tubers and roots will germinate and grow into food crops.

Subsequent to the plough the next fundamental device is the wheel. Carts and wagons displace sleds and pack-horses. Reaping machines on wheels took over from man-handled scythes and sickles at hay and corn harvest. Seed drills replaced sowing grain and small seeds by a fling of the hand with each stride of the sower. The pull of real live horse power turned the wheels of agricultural vehicles. The fuel was grass, hay and oats.

For a comparatively short period a companion provider of power on the land was the coal/wood fuelled steam traction engine. It was used to haul and drive the threshing machine. Working in pairs, opposite each other across a field they could winch a multi-furrow plough to and fro between them until, strip by strip, the land was ploughed. However, the horse was the supreme power force – the Shires, Clydesdales, Suffolk Punches and others, including the smaller Fell Ponies, Galloways and native breeds of hill and moor. Until wells of fuel-oil were discovered and the inevitable invention of the internal combustion engine.

The equine "Gentle Giants" and "rumbling, whirring steamers" became replaced by the horseless, roaring, compact tractors fuelled with petrol. The invention and adoption of automation is a consequence of man's inclination to avoid manual labour!

*Ploughing match*

*Steam power*

# 31

# ORGANIC

Early man realised that of what he harvested from the soil some remedial fertiliser must be returned. Just as in Nature, when vegetation decays (herbage, leaves, timber) it assimilates into soil and completes the cycle of nature "from earth to earth". Throughout the ages agricultural man has returned crop residue and animal manure to replenish the fertility from where he removed a crop. In so doing the soil has been regularly sustained with organic matter.

Organic farming is the long-time conventional system of agriculture. It followed a rotational cropping order, for example; in the initial stage the field is growing grass; so in the first year the field is ploughed and sown with a cereal (oats, wheat, barley etc). A harvest is taken off, and the remaining stubble ploughed in preparation for a root crop in the second year (potatoes, turnips, cabbage, kale etc). After the root crop is harvested the land is ploughed again and sown with a cereal for harvest in the third year, and undersown at the same time for a grass crop in the fourth year. When the hay is harvested the after-growth of grasses, known as fogg, returns the field to meadow for grazing whilst other fields on the farm take their turns in the rotation system. Root crops are grown on heavy applications of farmyard manure. Manure is also spread across grass fields when the decision is taken to raise a hay crop. The benefit of the yearly changes maintains humus and does not diminish fertility, whereas continual exclusive single cropping on average quality land results in time to a gradual decline in crop yield.

A big change in grassland management during the past half century is the widespread adoption of what is really an old-fashioned practice of mowing young grass before it becomes ripe enough to make hay and compress it into silage.

On some steeply situated fell side farms the buildings include a mowstead built into the side of the hill. This would be a situation where loads of new mown grass could be brought down from a hill-side meadow above the farmstead and dropped into the mowstead from an entry at the top. Inside it would be compressed by trampling (wearing strong, hob-nailed shepherd boots) and during winter dug out from an exit at the bottom farmyard level. Nowadays, the usual method is to clamp and "tractor roll" the grass in a prepared silage pit.

Fell farmers needed to be good hay makers. In our temperate climate of many weathers, a crop of ripening grass can be turned into sweet smelling hay during three days of warm sunshine and dry breeze. It may take as long as three weeks to enjoy the benefit of those three days, and three weeks might spread over three months from late June to early September!

Mown hay grass has to be conditioned. It has to be turned, and probably turned again until dry: made into haycocks (neat heaps) topped off shapely to lessen rain penetration. When rain threatened, fell farmers made smaller 'footcocks', each a neat fork full, rounded and capped, shapely. After rain footcocks could be easily shaken out to dry.

And for convenience the hay would be built into pikes; each either a cartload or a pike-bogie load, topped off to stand against rain and wind and also for "sweating out" moisture prior to being housed in barn or haystack. If stacked, then to be neatly capped with a thatch of straw or reeds (some described as cieves).

A younger generation of farmers has no experience of the trials and pleasures of making hay! They, unfortunately, have not breathed the pleasant smell of well-cut meadow hay. They know the smell of new mown tender grass (usually rye grasses) and they know the unpleasant smell of silage and the stink of slurry. But not all silage has a bad smell. Perhaps the most pleasant smelling is maize silage. And now maize for harvesting green is growing successfully even in Cumbria. The fragrance of well-got meadow hay is a memory to linger in the nostrils. The most delectable of all farmyard odours.

Other aspects of organic farming include the ploughing in of a specially sown green crop such as deep rooted red clover, also mustard. Growing turnips, kale and rape to be eaten off the land is known as the treatment of the "Golden Hoof" putting "management" into the soil.

Agricultural man observed a healthy growth of livestock pastured on limestone land. Consequently, where limestone could be quarried he crushed it and burnt it in kilns such as are still to be seen on the Bewcastle hills in Cumbria (reminders of a discarded task) and spread over his fields.

However, lime became very important during World War II when the Government Campaign to "plough and dig for Victory" revealed that much of our farmland was in dire need of a sweetener. Soil tests were taken everywhere and the Government sponsored a national lime spreading plan.

One of the busiest purveyors and contract spreaders of lime was a man called Adam Lythgoe with his Lancashire based company. This aspect of organic agriculture was at its most intensive. The pressure of war, shortage of food and life's essentials stimulated invention and a radical speed-up of work. Tractors with two-furrow plough, courageously imported from across the Atlantic Ocean through a submarine blockade of our islands, took over from pairs of horses with single furrow ploughs.

A big change in farming practice began. Whereas grass, hay and oats fuelled the horses, now imported petrol and paraffin fuelled the new, noisy and smelly tractors. Field operations became rushed.

During post war years more changes developed and the "unconventional" began to replace the traditional conventional. "Organic" was on its way out!

# 32

## THE NEW "CONVENTIONAL"

To increase crop production so-called "artificial" manures (what farmers call "bag muck") supplemented the effect of organic manure. These manures release nitrogen. If they are applied too heavily they kill off the plants and grasses which already release nitrogen naturally. The production of agricultural pharmaceuticals became a growth industry. Selective weed killers have taken over from work with hand and hoe. The first crop spraying operation I remember was on a crop of carrots. The usual hand weeding was accomplished by a group of "pocket-money-earning" school lads during a couple of hours after school or on a Saturday. This form of employment came to an end when the farmer discovered that a fine spray of paraffin oil killed the emerging weeds without affecting the carrots.

A fruit farmer in Kent told me of his first experience spraying pesticides to destroy aphids, greenfly, lice etc. His expectancy was that his orchard would be cleared of pests for a whole year, but discovered the need to spray three more times. He said, he had also killed off his friendly predators like the "lady birds" which are natural enemies of the aphids. It was good business for the pharmacists.

Selective weed killer sprays and powders are used to kill specific weeds without injuring the planted food crop. The ultimate systemic weed-killer destroys all plant life. It is used to clear land completely of all vegetation prior to being replanted or re-seeded in a weed-free soil. In political hands this weedkiller could be a "weapon of mass destruction", or to destroy illegally grown noxious plants.

Of course, when pesticides and herbicides were first adopted they were "unconventional". The conventional (traditional) system of weed control was as already described using hands and hoes. The conventional system included a tidy midden of farmyard manures – a steamy, hot monument to humus and fertility! Farmyard manure was carted on to the fields and unloaded in equal sized heaps at equal distances, placed conveniently to be evenly spread using a gripe. Weathered manure integrates into the soil where worms help the process. In modern practice manure is liquid, or very nearly liquid, and very clarty, called slurry. Slurry is applied as spray from a tractor-powered pressure tank. It pollutes rural air with a pungent stench. Heavy rainfall washes some of it into ditches and streams. Warm sunshine and dry winds harden the sludge into a crust.

In organic farming nitrogen is released through the natural agency of clover varieties and legumes, and promotes thick bottom grass growth essential for meadow grazing. Increased costs and low returns present farmers with a dilemma. The new "conventional" system is expensive and the financial returns unjustly low. It is difficult to break from this new, so-called "conventional" system, reliant upon chemicals, and stay in business. To help alleviate the problem is to choose a healthy diet from naturally and locally produced organic food. Then savour the flavour in comparison with the "flatness" of the same-named product in the fancy packet from the superstore.

The adoption of organic farming does not displace the machinery. No, the system requires to modify over-intensive methods and co-ordinate with former methods of ages-long experience, instead of promoting artificial forcing of crop growth, quick growth of beef cattle, dairy cows to produce many times more milk than their calves could need, fatter chickens for the table in a life of seven short weeks, confine pigs to cages to make lean bacon and pork! Such is factory farming!

# 33
# THE TWISTED SUBSIDY

During wartime, and immediate years following, both Government and populace appreciated the importance of agriculture. When food is scarce, and people hungry, farmers are popular. As much food as possible had to be grown from our own soil. The urge of Government was "Dig for Victory" and that basic tool, the ubiquitous plough earned the accolade a "weapon against hunger". Families queued for their weekly rations of food. For example, it was not until autumn of 1953 that rationing really ended when two ounces of cheese per person was doubled, thanks to a bonus consignment from Canada.

Since that time farming has undergone significant changes. In 1947 the British Government passed into law the "Agricultural Bill" to "promote a stable and efficient industry". It was described as a "curtain-raiser to a new era of farming policy in the interests of food producers and consumers". Farmers were promised guaranteed markets and prices that would ensure adequate return on capital invested.

This was cunningly arranged with a "consumer subsidy" intended to keep food prices low on the housewife's shopping bill. An Annual Price Review of farm products (including cereals, potatoes, milk, eggs, cattle sheep) to include a consumer subsidy more conveniently than to pay a subsidy directly to every household.

The subsidy payment scheme was to be a short-term measure (a long time ago!) but in the long-term, with problems, not entirely successful. One Member of Parliament accused the Government of "Feather bedding farmers". Fifty eight long term years later began the fading out of subsidy payments over a period of ten years. The subsidy payment for food ends but the payment in annually declining amounts continues to be paid to the farmers to compensate for their inherent traditional care of the countryside, ecology, environment, and the misleading "right to roam" over an "idyllic park"!

# 34

# FUNDAMENTAL CITIZENS

*Typical midday break finely portrayed in this sculpture by Border Fine Arts*

The fellowship of ploughmen is an unique world-wide experience. The spirit in which its purpose is embodied is universal. It is a spirit that exists as a natural gift among people whose fundamental labour is with the earth to produce food.

Methods and techniques differ according to climates and types of soil but the basic principal of tillage is the same now as it has been for thousands of years. Nevertheless, the soil is a mysterious and challenging thing and the common denominator uniting ploughers everywhere in the world is the fact that they all work with nature, and working with nature is an absorbing occupation. It imbues a lively interest in how every neighbour, near and far, meets the challenges of his own acres and of his own climate. There is a spirit of sympathy and understanding for one another's problems. There is even a desire to plough each other's fields together and test skills one with another. And that is what the World Ploughing Organisation makes possible.
In bringing together the best two ploughers of each country to plough the same field has a widespread influence over the farmlands of the world.

To compete in the World Contest is a great honour and achievement. Every competitor is a good plougher whatever his placing may be in the final result. He is one of the best ploughers in the world and his example will bear a great influence upon improving diligence and standard of work of others.

Every competitor in the World Ploughing Contest gained his entry solely because of his prowess with the plough. It is the simplest form of selection. No testimonials as to character, or certificates of education are asked for. There are no interviews before a board of selectors to assess the suitability of a competitor to represent his country or to examine his manners and behaviour and standard of intelligence. All the selecting is done by the plough. And the plough is very selective.

Farm workers, farmers' sons and farmers have been the participants in the Annual World Ploughing Contests since the first was held in Canada in 1953. Each rose to be a national champion plougher in his own country and every one has proved to be a credit to his country and to his profession. They have become ambassadors for world friendship and, without rhetoric or even knowing each other's verbal language, they have communicated happily and understandingly with each other.

They have met and impressed heads of Church and State, Presidents, Princes, Ministers and people and in each host country, dedicated a monument built of stone brought from each of their homelands to remind us that international understanding does clearly exist among the fundamental citizens who are the very centre of every nation – the ploughers and the farmers.

# 35
## Epilogue

*"Glencoyne" - a Cumbrian fell farm*

This book is associated with mountains and moors, valleys and lakes, rolling upland and plain. Such is the environment of the British Isles, encompassed by seas washing craggy coasts and sandy beaches; and swathed in a temperate climate.

From the air the countryside is a patchwork quilt of colourful enclosed fields interspersed with woods, forests, open moor and fell. Among the fields, in valleys and on fellsides are farmsteads ring-fenced by their respective hedge or stone dyke boundaries. Each holding is a food production unit where, variously, livestock graze, hens lay eggs, pigs become porkers. From the soil grow vegetables and cereals, and most important of all in our temperate climate, grass. Each farm house is the home of generation after generation of farming families. The buildings are byres for cows, styes for pigs, pens for sheep. There are poultry houses, dog kennels (the cats are independent and choose their own). Barns house harvested crops; sheds and workshops shelter farm machinery and the dairy holds the yield of twice-daily milking.

Each farm is employed in the husbandry of its soil, and the value of the farm is based upon the quality of the soil and the management applicable to its productive potential. Mountain and moorland breeds make good on mountain and moorland soils. Potatoes and sugar beet, downland sheep and cattle make good on plains soils. Soil is our most precious asset from which all land food crops emerge under the influence of sun, rain, wind and even frost.

Now, let us leave our ariel surveillance and make an earthbound expedition through our green and pleasant heritage land. Before long we realise there is no law that protects the preservation of long established productive farms, from being abolished – even demolished, done away with!

There are old houses and castles listed for preservation, but no safeguard list for an unique farmstead and land, long established both environmentally and ecologically, on a site of choice with regard to terrain, water, drainage, shelter, soil variety and every aspect of Nature that a pioneer farmer, during the Land Enclosure period, would have taken into consideration.

On our country travels, many times do we see that what was once a farm has now become a courtyard: a maze of house and ancillary buildings converted into attached dwellings for human beings. No moo of a cow, no bleat of a sheep, grunt of a pig or crowing of a cockerel. The farmyard a harbour of shiny motor cars. What of the land? The new occupants have no productive interest in it. Has it been hived off to other farms and/or sold to builders?

The crop rotation system may have been amalgamated with that of a neighbouring farm, or, perhaps more likely, become permanent grazing for the cattle or sheep of a "dog and stick" farmer?

When farms and farm folk disappear so does our prestigious livestock industry of healthy, pedigree breeds exported as foundation stock to many countries.

Already, a large proportion of the meat we eat – beef, mutton, chicken is imported from far-away places across oceans and continents. But the best is still being raised on our homeland farms. Farms that we still need and shall need (perhaps desperately) in the future. Please can we have the word "Agriculture" restored in place of that invented "Defra"? Also, keep the meaningful generic "Farmer" instead of the quango term "Land Manager". To be a farmer's boy: farming is the fundamental, immemorial profession and needs good practical farmers.